ALSO BY THE COOKING CLUB

THE COOKING CLUB COOKBOOK

THE COOKING CLUB PARTY COOKBOOK

THE COOKING CLUB

party

COOKBOOK

SIX FRIENDS SHOW YOU HOW TO DINE, DRINK, AND DISH

THE COOKING CLUB

KATHERINE FAUSSET

SHARON COHEN FREDMAN

REBECCA SAMPLE GERSTUNG

CYNTHIA HARRIS

LUCIA QUARTARARO MULDER

LISA SINGER

Photographs by Alexandra Rowley

VILLARD NEW YORK

DISCARD STAMFORD PUBLIC LIBRARY

Copyright © 2003 by Katherine Fausset, Sharon Cohen Fredman,
Rebecca Sample Gerstung, Cynthia Harris,
Lucia Quartararo Mulder, and Lisa Singer

All rights reserved under International and Pan-American Copyright
Conventions. Published in the United States by Villard Books,
an imprint of The Random House Publishing Group, a division
of Random House, Inc., New York, and simultaneously in
Canada by Random House of Canada Limited, Toronto.

VILLARD and "V" CIRCLED Design are registered
trademarks of Random House, Inc.

Library of Congress Cataloging-in-Publication Data

The Cooking Club party cookbook : six friends show you how to dine, drink,
and dish / The Cooking Club, Katherine Fausset . . . et al.].
p. cm.
ISBN 0-8129-6875-1
1. Entertaining.   2. Cookery.   I. Fausset, Katherine.   II. Cooking Club.
TX731.C645 2003
642'.4—dc21   2002044906

Villard Books website address: www.villard.com
Printed in China on acid-free paper

2 4 6 8 9 7 5 3

FIRST EDITION

Book design by Cynthia Harris
Food and prop styling by Cynthia Harris

3 3988 1003 4832 2

FOR OUR FRIENDS,
WHO GIVE US SO MANY REASONS TO CELEBRATE

THANK YOU

A toast to everyone who helped get this party started, in particular:

Greg Carr, Sheila and David McLean, and **Henry and Francine Rowley** for lending us their beautiful homes. **Hilary Black, Rosaliz Jimenez, Rob Kunsweiler, Claudia Woda,** and **Kay and Roy Fausset** at Judy at the Rink for party props and favors. **Janet Patry** for mixing some mean drinks. **Polly and Lee Sample** for driving the CC shuttle bus. **Tony Morgan, John Heil,** and the crew at the Blue Grotto for throwing *us* a great party.

Our culinary support group: **Andrea Aronson, Winnie Beattie, Jean Borrie, Georgia Close, Emily Bowen Cohen, Janet Cohen, Paula Derrow, Pam Drucker, Richard and Kim Fausset, Sally Fern, Winnie Flach, Eleni Gage, Wendy Gale, Bonnie Gerstung, Darren Gough, Ellen Hempling, Jack Hempling, Jenny Jacoby Hurd, Grace Goodyear Ingram-Eiser, Susan Kane, Nathan Lump, Leslie May, Alix McLean, Ellen Nyburg, Evie Poitevent, Anna Potter, Amanda Reeser, Robb Riedel, Jennifer Kaye Rowley, Allison and Niki Rubenstein, Debra Singer, Kelly Sutherlin, Sally Tusa,** and **Natasha Wimmer.** Special thanks to **Cynthia Rowley.**

Webdaddy **Ken Fredman** at S.O.T.A. Consulting for our website, www.cookingclub.net, and for keeping us laughing. **Steve Gerstung** for proudly wearing his CC T-shirt in a New Orleans bar. **Charlie Moran** for culinary and equestrian handicapping. Sous-chef and errand boy **Pieter Mulder** for his shrewd palate and hearty appetite.

The people that make it possible: **Mary Bahr, Jason Baruch, Todd Doughty, Lance Reynolds,** and **Claudia Cross.** And finally, **our parents and families** for giving us all the right ingredients.

CONTENTS

THE COOKING CLUB PARTY COOKBOOK

PARTY GIRLS

A year's worth of reasons to celebrate

MAYBE IT WAS THE PIÑATA that showed up at an otherwise ordinary Mexican dinner. Or that Sharon became pregnant and Lucia got engaged—in the same year. But something began to make Cooking Club's humble Sunday night suppers, well, a little more spectacular. For six years, we had been meeting once a month for a generous helping of home-cooked food and much-needed downtime. But suddenly we had major milestones to celebrate. To honor the impending arrival of our newest member, Sharon's daughter, Margot Sydney, we borrowed some pretty pink china for a tea party and made our menu pint-size: mini scones, dainty sandwiches, and baby cakes. When Lucia and Pieter got engaged, we thought it only fitting that we treat them to a culinary trip to Paris, the city of love, with Kir Royales and French crepes. We became so accustomed to entertaining that even when we didn't have a holiday or special day to commemorate, we celebrated anyway. Just because.

After years of facing the Cooking Club test kitchen, we found that our bona fide catastrophes became fewer and farther between. So here we are with book two, a compendium of our parties and celebrations. In the course of all this entertaining, we've developed a few ideas for keeping the focus on the fun and not the formality. These tips haven't been vetted by the etiquette police or cross-referenced with any professional entertaining gurus. They're just our thoughts about what makes a party special—not perfect. Let us know what you think at our website: www.cookingclub.net.

I FIND A REASON TO THROW A PARTY It's not hard, trust us. In all the years we've been together, finding an excuse to eat, drink, and be merry has never been a problem. We've feted one another's birthdays, chowed down while watching the Oscars, and christened one another's new apartments. And although we've had our share of major holiday celebration (our Fourth of July party featured Katherine's grilled-veggie-kabob-twirling act), we don't limit ourselves to those, and neither should you. Think outside of the calendar box—anything is fair game. If you're experiencing a culinary block, there is always a national holiday to celebrate—literally. It might not be in your Filofax, but February 4 is Homemade Soup Day, April 20 is the World Grits Festival, and November 3 is National Sandwich Day. Bottom line: Anything can be spun into a party; the important thing is getting together. And sometimes, that's reason enough.

2 DON'T OVERPLAN Why is it always the parties with the big buildup that leave us feeling as empty as a picked-over platter of cocktail shrimp? Sometimes the promise of an all-hours open bar, the monthlong quest for a cute outfit, and—dare we say it—ice sculptures only lead to one thing: party letdown. Think back to high school, when the preparty of hair-curling and eye-shadowing in the bathroom with your girlfriends was more fun than the actual event. Inevitably, Mr. I'm-too-cool-to-ask-you-to-dance ignored you and left you no alternative but to head back to your girlfriend's house, where you'd bake an emergency batch of Rice Krispie treats and crank up the Madonna. And that's when the *real* party started! You found that unopened bottle of peach schnapps, and . . . well, OK, so maybe that wasn't exactly how it happened for you, but you get the idea. The heart of the party comes from the people, not the planning.

3 HAVE A COHOST—OR FIVE If you've ever thrown a dinner party solo, you know what a stress-fest it can be (and we're not even talking about planning what to wear). That's

introduction

why our best parties have been the ones that we've collectively thrown. As the saying goes, many hands make for light work. Plus, there's the built-in clause that even if no one else shows up, you automatically have five guests. If you divvy up the workload, it won't seem like work at all. Decorating duties, lighting schemes, any planned art installations, and cleanup should be split up. As for what to wear, well, you're on your own.

4 FIND A SPACE, ANY SPACE Just because you don't own a penthouse apartment with a gold cupola doesn't mean you can't throw a fabulous party. Mansion, apartment, shack, or hut—you can make any space into a great place to celebrate. For our Chinese New Year dinner, the six of us piled into Cynthia's tiny Chinatown apartment and gave new meaning to eating "family style." Also, get creative with the space you've got. Don't have room for a big dining room table? Throw pillows on the floor and have a casual brunch like the one we had on New Year's Day. (We loved eating while lounging on pillows, even though a sleepy Becky promptly passed out after a few bites of Almond Croissant French Toast [page 151] and got syrup in her hair.)

5 CREATE A GUEST LIST—SIZE DOESN'T MATTER Whether it's your whole neighborhood, your cooking club, or just a few friends, all a party make. This book gives you twelve different causes for cooking and celebration, but let's get one thing straight: Unless you really enjoy vacuuming, you probably don't want to entertain hordes of people at home twelve times a year. That's why we've designed our themes for small or large get-togethers. In fact, we've had most of these parties with just the six of us, although for a few, like our Halloween party, we probably should have invited guests. Lucia discovered the hard way that there's nothing sadder than spending hours on a Sir Lancelot costume only to have five other people appreciate it, and only one person (Katherine, who came as a pirate) to joust with. But smaller gatherings are just as much fun and certainly less of a hassle.

THE COOKING CLUB PARTY COOKBOOK

6 DON'T STRESS The most important advice we can give you is to enjoy yourself. Why are you doing this after all? Certainly not for your health, as our Far-Out Fried Fondue (page 98) recipe proves. You're doing it for fun. Lisa didn't get upset when a colony of ants marched on her linzer squares during our picnic. Instead, she rallied the troops to the pool and started an impromptu synchronized swimming competition. So if you're cooking for Columbus Day and your meatballs fall apart, don't worry. Turn your company's attention to *The Sopranos* and whip up a Bolognese sauce that would make any godfather proud.

7 SET THE MOOD Want a surefire way to transform your dinner into a party? Well, then buy, rent, or borrow some decorations to match the theme. For our '70s fondue party, Becky was determined to bring a funkadelic orange beanbag chair from a friend's apartment. (Unfortunately for her husband, Steve, she didn't register its massive size until he was hauling it—on his head—through the streets of Manhattan.) But you don't have to deck the halls from top to bottom for success. A few key details—think jack-o'-lanterns for Halloween or red roses at a Kentucky Derby party—can make all the difference. And don't be afraid to dress the part. Not only did we unearth some relics from our own wardrobes, but we hit up our friends and families for their stash of festive wear. We scored a supersize sombrero for our Cinco de Mayo fiesta, and Sharon donated her wedding veil for Lucia's bachelorette party.

introduction

8 DOCUMENT THE EVENT We've found that when putting forth the extra effort that a theme party requires, it's really worth capturing key moments with a few snapshots. The fact that we missed the chance to immortalize six-months-pregnant Sharon as she swatted a piñata with a broomstick still pains us. It's also a great idea to keep a binder filled with your favorite recipes from past parties. Not only will you then be able to re-create your beloved bouillabaisse at a moment's notice, but you'll also wind up with a scrapbook full of successful menus.

9 MAKE USE OF THE READY-MADE Throwing your party solo? Not a problem—help awaits in aisle three. Don't worry, we'd never tell. Our Filly Cheese Sticks (page 62) are a perfect example—bake frozen puff-pastry dough with cheddar and spices, and the result beats a bag of Chee-tos any day. Plus, your guests won't suffer the fate of unnaturally orange fingertips. Another idea: Try store-bought pesto tossed with fresh tomatoes and fancy pasta—suddenly you have food to feed the in-laws, and all you did was boil water.

10 CHOOSE DISHES THAT YOU CAN PREPARE AHEAD That means no to risotto, unless you want to install bleachers in your kitchen for guests to watch. If you really get a charge out of flexing your culinary muscles in public, then by all means chain yourself to the stove. But some dishes, such as our Papaya-Honeydew Pico de Gallo (page 51) or Judy's Chicken Salad with Mango Chutney (page 87), taste even better if you make them in advance. In fact, if you put your mind to it (or just ask your two Texan aunts, like Katherine did for our Make-Ahead Margaritas on page 55), there's usually a way to adapt any recipe so that you can spend your party time on more essential endeavors—like introducing the adorable guy from your office to single club members.

11 OR . . . TRY MAKING THE PREP PART OF THE PARTY Why do people always migrate to the kitchen at a party? It's either the fridge full of cold beer, or they just want to be where the action is. So don't make your guilt-ridden guests stand there and timidly ask, "You don't need any help, right?" Make cooking the main event. For our crepe parties (see page 34), we flip a bunch ahead of time and keep them warm in the oven. Then, when guests arrive, we let everybody have a try at making one. It's a guaranteed conversation starter, and at how many parties do *you* get to master a French culinary skill? But a little advance preparation goes a long way toward ensuring that your kitchen doesn't look like the aftermath of a tropical storm. Clean up the batter from the preparty flipping that has

hardened into an abstract 3-D pattern on your range, and keep a nice clean bowl of batter for guests to try. Our make-your-own pizza (page 114) is another great option—place all chopped, sliced, grated toppings in separate bowls for easy access.

12 CELEBRATE—AS OFTEN AS POSSIBLE Some of our favorite parties have been the ones that were spun out of a need to infuse some cheer into a gloomy Sunday night. When Punxsutawney Phil glimpsed his shadow, damning us to six more weeks of winter, did we mope? No. We grabbed our resort wear, bought some tropical lawn chairs, and took the bus out to New Jersey for a midwinter luau at Sharon's house. Sure, it's easier to celebrate when you've got a newly engaged friend who needs to be hazed with a karaoke bachelorette party, or another who's on the precipice of motherhood. But what's kept our club together for more than six years is that at the end of a cold, wet trek below Houston Street on a blustery New York night, there's the warmth of a dinner with friends.

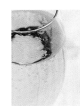

introduction

CASHEW CHICKEN AND
BOK CHOY GARDEN STIR-FRY

chinese new year

MENU

LONG-LIFE NOODLE SOUP

SHRIMP SPRING ROLLS WITH
SWEET-AND-SOUR DIPPING SAUCE

CASHEW CHICKEN

BOK CHOY GARDEN STIR-FRY

LUCKY WHOLE FISH

FORTUNE COOKIES

MEAL OF FORTUNE

A Chinese feast for the Year of the Pig-Out

WITH OUR JANUARY RESOLUTIONS long since frozen over, February for Cooking Club is a welcome chance for a fresh start. Just follow the crackle of fireworks south of Canal Street in New York City, and you'll see what we mean. Based on the lunar calendar, Chinese New Year is actually a fifteen-day-long celebration chock-full of traditions, superstitions, and feasting. Though some authentic dishes include daunting ingredients such as cloud ear fungus and black moss, there are many more that are easy to prepare and might make you reconsider take-out for good. One important note: In China, food is imbued with symbolic meaning, so what you eat and how you eat it is believed to directly affect your fortunes for the coming year. How's that for pressure?

According to the legend of the holiday, in ancient times there lived a scary monster named Niam, who would gobble up villagers every New Year. Needless to say, there wasn't much cause for celebration, until a wise old man announced that this monster could be scared off by loud noises and the color red. Thus, every year, firecrackers are lit, and people dress and decorate with the color red, to keep Niam (now the modern Chinese word for "year") at bay. Lisa, the most superstitious member of Cooking Club, was intrigued and circulated an e-mail primer of New Year's customs and taboos that would ensure us a safe and prosperous year. (How'd we do? See our scorecard on the right.)

We figured that Cynthia's Chinatown digs would be fitting for both atmosphere and last-minute bok choy runs, and decided that each dish should be a traditional part of the

New Year's menu, with the sole exception of dessert. Although we couldn't resist making them, fortune cookies, we learned, are about as Chinese as Fig Newtons.

Our Cooking Club Chinese New Year could not be complete without a nod to the Kitchen God, a Chinese deity to whom we figured we'd better pay homage. In Chinese homes, his paper image is hung year-round above the stove and then burned annually on the New Year. But what the Kitchen God looked like was a mystery to us. Who could embody this being who supposedly watches over our domestic affairs all year long? After some debate over whether a picture of the Pillsbury Doughboy or of Julia Child was an appropriate stand-in, we noticed that Cynthia already had a picture of the six of us taped to the cabinet above the stove. And we thought to ourselves, if one kitchen god was enough to watch over an entire household, surely six Kitchen Goddesses were even better.

SUPERSTITION SAVVY

DON'T CLEAN THE HOUSE: It's said that if you sweep dirt and dust out the door, you sweep out good fortune, and quite possibly a family member. Any excuse not to sweep was fine by us.

AVOID ALL SHARP THINGS: No knives or scissors can be used, lest your fortune be "cut off." This means no to haircuts, so Becky grudgingly canceled her color and trim, once we reminded her about the monster Niam.

NO FOUL LANGUAGE: While carrying heavy casserole pots up to a fifth-floor walk-up, we found this to be perhaps our greatest challenge.

DO NOT GREET ANYBODY IN THEIR BEDROOM: Hmmm. Although Cynthia usually greets us draped in a silk cheongsam from her bed, she was forced to refrain just this once.

EXCHANGE RED PAPER ENVELOPES WITH MONEY: Sharon filled ours with foil-wrapped chocolate coins, which looked suspiciously like the Hanukkah ones she brought to Holiday Cooking Club.

ALL DEBTS MUST BE PAID: Finally, a guilty Lucia caved and returned Lisa's grill pan that was "borrowed" three years ago.

LONG-LIFE NOODLE SOUP

The Chinese invented the noodle (it's thanks to Marco Polo that the Italians ever got hold of it). Traditionally, the longer the noodle, the better, as eating long noodles is believed to ensure a long life. In China, soups are served very hot, and it's OK to bring the bowl to your mouth, using chopsticks to shovel the noodles in. Slurping sounds are also OK, which makes us wonder what Chinese children get in trouble for at the dinner table. ■ *Yield: 4 to 6 servings*

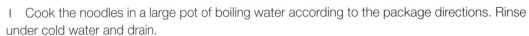

6 ounces long Chinese wheat noodles
(you can substitute almost any long noodle)

4 dried shiitake mushrooms

1 tablespoon soy sauce

½ teaspoon firmly packed light brown sugar

1 teaspoon salt

2 teaspoons rice wine or dry sherry

1½ teaspoons sesame oil

¼ teaspoon chili sauce

5 cups chicken broth

2 tablespoons plus 1 teaspoon vegetable oil

4 scallions (white parts plus
2 inches of green), minced

2 thin slices (⅛ inch thick, about the
size of a quarter) peeled fresh ginger

½ cup cooked 1- to 2-inch-long,
thin strips of pork, beef, or chicken

⅓ cup soybean or mung bean sprouts,
washed and drained

⅓ cup canned sliced bamboo shoots,
drained and julienned

1 cup shredded iceberg lettuce

I   Cook the noodles in a large pot of boiling water according to the package directions. Rinse under cold water and drain.

2   Soak the mushrooms in hot water until softened. Squeeze dry and remove any hard stems. Slice thinly.

3   In a small bowl, combine the soy sauce, sugar, salt, and wine with ½ teaspoon sesame oil and the chili sauce. Stir well.

4   Heat the chicken broth in a large saucepan or stockpot and keep it warm on the stove.

5   In a wok or large skillet, heat 1 teaspoon each of the sesame and vegetable oils over high heat. Add the noodles and quickly stir-fry for about 1 minute. Remove from the heat and divide the noodles into individual serving bowls.

6   Heat 2 tablespoons of vegetable oil in the wok or large skillet until very hot but not smoking. Add the scallions (leaving some for garnish), the ginger, and the meat, and stir-fry for about 1 minute. Add the mushrooms, sprouts, bamboo shoots, and lettuce, and stir-fry for another minute. Stir in the soy sauce mixture and combine until all the ingredients are well coated. Spoon over the noodles in the individual bowls.

7   Bring the broth almost to a boil, pour it into the bowls, and garnish with scallions.

THE COOKING CLUB PARTY COOKBOOK

ORANGES AND TANGERINES, SYMBOLIZING WEALTH AND GOOD FORTUNE, MAKE AN EASY (AND EDIBLE) CENTERPIECE

SHRIMP SPRING ROLLS WITH
SWEET-AND-SOUR DIPPING SAUCE

It's thought that golden-brown spring rolls look enough like stacked-up gold bricks to ensure you wealth in the year ahead. Does it follow that the more spring rolls you eat, the more money you get? We'll let you decide. ▪ *Yield: 10 spring rolls*

FOR THE SAUCE
⅓ cup rice wine or white wine vinegar
2 teaspoons cornstarch
⅓ cup firmly packed light brown sugar
⅓ cup water
¼ teaspoon salt
1 tablespoon ketchup

FOR THE SPRING ROLLS
2 teaspoons sesame oil
4 cups plus 1 tablespoon
vegetable oil
2 cloves garlic, minced

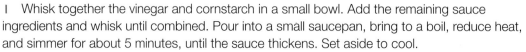

1 pound small shrimp, peeled and deveined
(or cut larger shrimp into halves or thirds)
2 teaspoons minced fresh ginger
4 cups shredded Chinese or napa cabbage
(iceberg lettuce can be substituted)
1 cup soybean or mung bean sprouts,
washed and drained
1 tablespoon soy sauce
1 tablespoon hoisin sauce
1 tablespoon rice wine or dry sherry
½ teaspoon salt
10 frozen egg or spring roll wrappers, thawed
1 egg, beaten

1   Whisk together the vinegar and cornstarch in a small bowl. Add the remaining sauce ingredients and whisk until combined. Pour into a small saucepan, bring to a boil, reduce heat, and simmer for about 5 minutes, until the sauce thickens. Set aside to cool.

2   Heat 1 teaspoon sesame oil and 1 tablespoon vegetable oil in a wok or large skillet, until very hot. Add the garlic and stir a few seconds, until fragrant. Add the shrimp and stir-fry for about 3 minutes, until bright pink on all sides. Remove the shrimp from the wok and set aside.

3   Add 1 teaspoon sesame oil to the wok and cook over medium-high heat. Add the ginger; stir-fry a few seconds, until fragrant. Add the cabbage, sprouts, soy sauce, hoisin sauce, wine, and salt; stir-fry for about 2 minutes. Return the shrimp to the pan, stir-fry for 1 minute more, then, using a slotted spoon to drain off any excess liquid, transfer the mixture to a bowl.

4   Clean and dry the wok and begin heating 4 cups vegetable oil in it, to 375 degrees.

5   Lay a wrapper on a cutting board with one corner pointing toward you. Place 2 heaping tablespoons of the filling in a log shape along the center of the wrapper. Brush the edges of the wrapper with the beaten egg. Roll the wrapper over the filling once, fold in the sides, then roll like a jelly roll all the way and seal the edges. Continue making all the rolls.

6   Deep-fry the rolls until golden brown. Remove and drain on paper towels; serve with sauce.

CASHEW CHICKEN

The yin-yang of opposing flavors and textures is a principle of Chinese cooking. Here the crunch of cashews and water chestnuts combined with tender chicken is a delicious example of that. You're technically supposed to serve a whole chicken, complete with head, feet, and tail, for New Year's, but we just couldn't bring ourselves to do it. Aren't you glad? ■ *Yield: 4 servings, or 6 as part of a multi-course meal*

2 tablespoons cornstarch

2 tablespoons soy sauce

2 tablespoons hoisin sauce

3 tablespoons water

¼ teaspoon sesame oil

1 tablespoon rice wine or dry sherry

1½ pounds boneless, skinless chicken breasts, rinsed and patted dry with paper towels, cut into 1-inch cubes

1 tablespoon peanut or vegetable oil

2 cloves garlic, minced

1 teaspoon minced fresh ginger

½ cup canned sliced water chestnuts, drained

3 scallions (white parts plus 2 inches of green), sliced on the diagonal

¾ cup unsalted cashews

½ cup canned chicken broth

1 In a small bowl, whisk the cornstarch, soy sauce, hoisin sauce, water, sesame oil, and wine.

2 Place the chicken cubes in a bowl and coat them with half of the sauce. Set aside.

3 Heat the peanut oil in a wok or large skillet until very hot but not smoking. Add the garlic and ginger, and stir-fry for 30 seconds, then add the chicken. Cook, stirring occasionally, until all sides are lightly browned but not cooked through, about 3 to 4 minutes.

4 Add the water chestnuts, scallions, cashews, remaining sauce, and chicken broth and stir until well coated. Cook for a few minutes more, until the sauce thickens. Serve immediately.

chinese new year

BOK CHOY GARDEN STIR-FRY

An everyday Chinese vegetable, bok choy is essential to a New Year dinner. Look for it either in its regular large size or in small bunches known as baby bok choy. Cynthia, always eager for a crafts project, has actually been whittling away these carrot flowers since high school, when all she wanted for Christmas was a wok. She eventually got one, but you don't have to. A large skillet works just fine. ■ *Yield: 4 servings*

2 large carrots
1 pound bok choy, or about 4 bunches baby bok choy
¼ cup canned chicken broth
1 tablespoon soy sauce
1 teaspoon cornstarch
½ teaspoon sugar
¼ teaspoon salt
1 tablespoon vegetable oil
1 teaspoon sesame oil
2 cloves garlic, minced
½ teaspoon salt

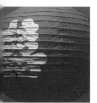

1   To prepare the carrots (see photo at right), peel them and, using a sharp knife, make a shallow cut, only about ½ inch deep, along the entire length of the carrot. Make a second cut right next to it so that you are cutting out a sliver of carrot. Continue all the way around the carrot, then slice the carrot about ¼ inch thick to make the flower shape.
2   Boil the carrot slices for about 5 minutes; drain. Set the carrots aside.
3   Trim the bottom of each bok choy bunch, separate the leaves, wash and dry well, and cut into 2-inch pieces.
4   In a small bowl, whisk together the broth, soy sauce, cornstarch, sugar, and salt. Set aside.
5   Heat the vegetable and sesame oils in a wok or large skillet until very hot but not smoking. Add the garlic and stir-fry briefly, about 30 seconds. Add the bok choy and stir-fry on high heat for 1 minute, until the bok choy reduces in volume. Add the sauce and continue to stir-fry for about 2 minutes. Serve.

SHANGHAI SURPRISE:
THESE CARROT
FLOWERS ARE A
CINCH TO MAKE

LUCKY WHOLE FISH

To ensure a prosperous new year, a steamed whole fish is traditionally eaten, but it raised some debate within the Cooking Club. Lisa doesn't like a fish eye looking back at her while she's eating, and navigating the sea of tiny bones proved tricky for everybody. So we offer this dish up two ways: the whole fish for traditionalists and the option to use fillets. ■ *Yield: 4 to 6 servings*

salt and freshly ground pepper to taste

1 fresh whole fish such as red snapper or sea bass
(approximately 3 pounds), cleaned and gutted (most fish
stores will do this), or 1½ pounds fish fillets or steaks

8 to 10 leaves of Chinese or napa cabbage, cut into quarters
(regular green cabbage can be substituted)

5 scallions (white parts plus 2 inches of green)

¼ cup fresh lemon juice

1 clove garlic, minced

1 teaspoon sesame oil

1 tablespoon peanut or vegetable oil

1 tablespoon fish sauce

1 tablespoon soy sauce

dash cayenne pepper

1 heaping tablespoon minced peeled fresh ginger

1 tablespoon minced fresh cilantro

1 Preheat the oven to 450 degrees.

2 Rinse the fish inside and out and pat it dry with a paper towel. Salt and pepper the fish, and place it on a bed of cabbage in the center of a large piece of aluminum foil on a baking sheet.

3 Mince 1 scallion.

4 In a small bowl, combine the lemon juice, garlic, sesame and peanut oils, fish sauce, soy sauce, cayenne pepper, ginger, cilantro, and minced scallion.

5 Mince the remaining scallions. If using a whole fish, brush the inside of the fish with one third of the sauce, stuff the scallions into the fish cavity, and brush the fish with or pour on the rest of the sauce. Seal in foil. If using fillets, pour the sauce over the fillets, sprinkle with the chopped scallions, and seal in foil. Bake the fish for 30 to 45 minutes, depending on the thickness, until it is white and flakes easily with a fork.

6 Unwrap the foil and place the whole fish and the cooked cabbage on a serving platter, or if using fillets, on individual plates as desired.

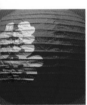

FORTUNE COOKIES

After making your own fortune cookies, you will have newfound respect for the cellophane-wrapped kind. The challenge is that you have to fold them while they're hot (they harden quickly), so we recommend doing one at a time until you get the hang of it. Or better yet, get a couple of your fellow club members to help fold immediately as the cookies come out of the oven. Watch the elbows, though, and no peeking at the fortunes! ■ *Yield: about 10 cookies*

2 egg whites
¼ teaspoon almond extract
¼ teaspoon ground ginger
¼ cup all-purpose flour
⅓ cup sugar

WHAT YOU'LL NEED READY: a spatula, a thick dishcloth to protect your hands from the hot cookies, a wooden spoon, and a muffin tin, which is helpful but not essential for cooling the cookies individually.

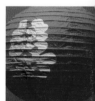

1 Write your fortunes on thin strips of paper using nontoxic ink.
2 Preheat the oven to 400 degrees.
3 Whisk the egg whites until foamy. Gradually add the remaining ingredients and continue to whisk until well combined.
4 On a greased baking sheet, pour 1 tablespoon of batter and gently spread out the batter with the back of a spoon, forming a circle about 3 inches in diameter.
5 Bake for 5 minutes, or until the edges are brown but the center of the cookie is still pale.
6 Don't panic! Just slide a spatula under the hot cookie and place it (pan side down) on your dishtowel-covered hand. Place the fortune across the center of the circle, fold the cookie in half, and with your thumb and forefinger gently press the top edges together, leaving the center of the cookie puffed out, fortune inside. Allow the cookie to harden for about 10 seconds, then bend the sides of the cookie over the handle of a wooden spoon to create the classic fortune cookie shape. Hold the cookie in place about 10 more seconds, then place it in a muffin tin or bowl, to allow it to hold its shape while cooling.
7 Go back to step four, and continue until you've used up all the batter. (**NOTE:** Cookies can be made in advance and stored in an airtight container or Ziploc bag until needed.)

chinese new year

LUAU LAVA FLOWS AND
HAWAIIAN PUNCH MAI TAIS

hawaiian luau

MENU

LOMI LOMI SALMON

KALUA CHICKEN WITH
HAWAIIAN BARBECUE SAUCE

MAHI MAHI WITH MANGO SALSA

CRUNCHY KAUAI
MACADAMIA-NUT COOKIES

LUAU LAVA FLOWS

HAWAIIAN PUNCH MAI TAIS

HAWAII FIVE BELOW

We warm up with a midwinter luau

IT ALL STARTED WITH THE "resort wear" section at Saks. As Katherine was shopping to replace her favorite boots (the heel had broken off in a freak incident involving acorn squash), she bumped into the racks of sarongs, bikinis, and shorts all targeted at shoppers planning a winter jaunt to Saint Bart's. That night, after filling us in on her boot fiasco, she lamented the callousness of stores that taunt us with warm-weather wear when most of us have no plans to be in the sun. As Sharon told us about the vacation that she and Ken had just spent in Hawaii, our next Cooking Club celebration became clear: a midwinter luau.

For the native Hawaiian, a luau is a time for family and friends to hang loose, listening to hula music while sharing folklore. Although the word *luau* literally means "feast," the food at these festivities takes a backseat to the intoxicating fruity drinks. Since a luau can be celebrated at any time and for any occasion, we dug our strappy sandals out of the closet (Katherine gave her new boots the evening off) and threw on the fresh orchid leis that Cynthia ordered online. Becky showed up with two bright red Hawaiian-print beach chairs that she bought without once considering what to do with them afterward. And Sharon sent Ken out on a mission to find fresh coconuts so we could all have the authentic experience of drinking out of one. Before we knew it, Becky was strumming on our new ukulele and singing Don Ho tunes as the rest of us were hamming it up and hula dancing.

Speaking of ham . . . traditionally, a whole pig is roasted all day in an imu pit (a large hole used as an underground oven) and unveiled to luau guests before the meat is peeled and made into a dish called kalua pork (similar to jerk chicken). Apartment living, among many other obvious obstacles, made this typical luau fare out of the question for us. So Sharon substituted chicken for pork, and used aluminum foil and her oven to create kalua chicken. Of course, if you want to dig a pit in your backyard and bury a pig, we're not stopping you, although we're pretty sure your neighbors, if not the local police, might.

Poi, another luau staple, is taro root that has been pounded into a thick purple pulp. We said "P-U" to poi. We also took liberties with other luau dishes by infusing our favorite foods (such as cookies and salsa) with traditional Hawaiian fare such as macadamia nuts and mangoes. And since the biggest draw for going to a luau in Hawaii is the "all you can drink" policy, we also made two delectable drinks, which is probably how we found ourselves praying to the tiki statues Cynthia borrowed from her parents' basement before the night was done. Aloha!

TIKI TIPS

1. **START DECORATING:** Nothing is over the top at a luau—inflatable palm trees, seashells, beach chairs, and ukuleles are all acceptable. Stock up on tropical fruit for exotic centerpieces. Create mood lighting with candles, tiki torches, or paper lanterns. Large leaves can be used either as plates or to display food, and don't forget little umbrella toothpicks. Another essential: Hawaiian music. Although these items are easier to find in the summer, they can all be ordered off the Internet any time of year.

2. **DRESS THE PART:** This is the only time that a grass skirt or coconut bra will be acceptable attire. And break out the outfit you bought on vacation but later realized could only be seen at a Jimmy Buffett concert. And it goes without saying that each guest *must* get "lei'd" as they walk in the door.

3. **BUY ORCHIDS:** They can be pricey, but buying a few will be worth the expense. They can be used loose as a garnish for food and drinks, floated with candles as a table centerpiece, or even as a hair accessory. The tradition is that if you are single, the flower should be worn behind the right ear; and if you are taken, it should be worn behind the left ear. Rumor has it that these flowers are even edible, although don't look here for confirmation.

LOMI LOMI SALMON

The meaning of the word *lomi* in Hawaiian is "massage." It's an appropriate name for this appetizer because the easiest way to combine this mixture of salted raw salmon (we cheated and used lox), diced onions, and tomatoes is with your hands—like a massage. Lomi lomi salmon is delicious served chilled over ice, in a scooped-out tomato or pepper, even on a cracker. Sharon's husband mixed the leftovers in his eggs, making a Hawaiian omelette. ▪ *Yield: 6 to 8 servings*

½ pound smoked salmon
4 tomatoes, seeded and cubed
1 large onion, chopped
2 scallions (white parts plus 2 inches of green), chopped
1 teaspoon fresh lemon juice
salt and freshly ground pepper to taste
red pepper flakes (optional)

1　Shred the salmon into ½-inch pieces.
2　In a medium bowl, combine the rest of the ingredients.
3　Add the salmon to the vegetable mixture and stir well (the best way to get the salmon evenly distributed is by using your hands). Chill before serving.

KALUA CHICKEN WITH HAWAIIAN BARBECUE SAUCE

At Hawaiian luaus, a pig is seasoned with sea salt and placed in a 5-foot-deep hole (called an imu pit) that's lined with lava rocks, which produce a smoky flavor called kalua and a tender meat easy to peel. Usually kalua meats don't require any sauces (the cooking process alone produces plenty of moisture and flavor), but our ovens can't produce this smoky flavor, so we paired the pulled chicken with our version of a Hawaiian barbecue sauce. ■ *Yield: 6 servings*

FOR THE CHICKEN
1 teaspoon sea salt
(iodized salt can be substituted)
3 pounds chicken breast
(rinsed and patted dry with paper towels)

FOR THE SAUCE
1 cup ketchup
½ cup honey

2 tablespoons white vinegar
2 tablespoons mustard
1 tablespoon brown sugar
1 tablespoon Worcestershire sauce
1 teaspoon Tabasco Sauce
2 cloves garlic, minced
salt and freshly ground pepper to taste

1 Preheat the oven to 350 degrees.

2 To make the chicken, season with salt. Prepare three separate aluminum foil packets and divide the chicken into equal parts (about 1 pound per foil packet). Wrap the chicken in foil, making sure to seal all ends tightly so steam can't escape and juices can't leak. (Tip: Wrap once, then turn the packet upside down and wrap a second time with more foil.)

3 Put the packets in a roasting dish to avoid leaks and bake them for an hour.

4 To make the sauce, combine all the ingredients in a saucepan. Bring to a boil over medium heat. Reduce the heat and simmer for 10 minutes. Cover and refrigerate until the sauce thickens.

5 Remove the chicken from the oven and open the packets. Warning: The steam is very hot. It is easier to use scissors to open the packets.

6 Once the chicken is cool enough to handle, take the tender chicken and shred it with your hands into bite-size pieces. Serve it with sauce on the side for dipping.

hawaiian luau

MAHI MAHI WITH
MANGO SALSA

MAHI MAHI WITH MANGO SALSA

A little trivia: Dolphin is the real name of the fish we call mahi mahi, but this fish is not the mammal we also call dolphin. To avoid confusion, most restaurants use the Hawaiian name mahi mahi so customers don't think they're being served Flipper. Smart! Whatever it's called, we simply put this fish on the grill (Sharon conveniently has one on her balcony, which we find any excuse to use all year long), then combine it with a mango puree and mango salsa to create a beautiful dish.

■ *Yield: 4 servings*

FOR THE PUREE
1 mango, peeled and cut into chunks
2 to 3 tablespoons cold water
½ teaspoon sugar
salt and freshly ground pepper to taste

FOR THE SALSA
1 mango, peeled and cut into small pieces
1 small onion, diced
½ red bell pepper, seeded and diced
½ orange bell pepper, seeded and diced
½ green bell pepper, seeded and diced
½ yellow bell pepper, seeded and diced
2 to 3 scallions (white parts plus 2 inches of green), chopped
1 tablespoon minced fresh cilantro
3 tablespoons fresh lime juice

—

2 pounds mahi mahi

hawaiian luau

1　Combine the puree ingredients in a blender and puree until smooth. Chill.
2　Combine the remaining ingredients, except the mahi mahi. Refrigerate for at least 30 minutes before serving, to allow the flavors to develop.
3　Grill the mahi mahi for a few minutes on each side. Do not overcook, to prevent the fish from getting too dry. (Another alternative is to cook the mahi mahi in a skillet with olive oil.)
4　Pour the mango puree on individual plates or a platter. (Here's your chance to be decorative with your food.)
5　Set the mahi mahi on the puree, and top with the salsa.

CRUNCHY KAUAI MACADAMIA-NUT COOKIES

Having spent a semester of college in Sydney, Becky spilled the beans about the origins of the macadamia nut. The macadamia tree was discovered in the land down under, not in the islands of aloha. Then the seeds from this Australian tree were planted on the fertile, subtropic shores of Hawaii, where this tasty nut flourished, leaving Aussies with only Vegemite to call their own.

■ *Yield: 4 to 5 dozen cookies*

16 tablespoons (2 sticks) unsalted butter, softened
½ cup sugar
1 cup firmly packed light brown sugar
2 eggs
2 teaspoons vanilla extract
2½ cups all-purpose flour
1 teaspoon baking soda
½ teaspoon salt
1 11- or 12-ounce bag white chocolate chips
6 ounces macadamia nuts, coarsely chopped

1 Preheat the oven to 350 degrees.
2 Using an electric mixer, cream the butter and sugars in a large bowl. Add the eggs and vanilla extract, and mix.
3 In a medium bowl, combine the flour, baking soda, and salt.
4 Add the flour mixture to the butter mixture, and stir until the dry ingredients dissolve.
5 Stir in the chips and nuts.
6 Make balls of dough (each ball should be approximately 1 tablespoon) and place them on lightly greased cookie sheets.
7 Bake for 15 minutes, until the cookies are golden brown.

PUNCH DRUNK: LISA (LEFT) AND LUCIA AFTER ONE TOO MANY MAI TAIS

LUAU LAVA FLOWS

If you like piña coladas and getting caught in the rain, then you must have already sucked down too many Lava Flows. If you're in a rush, you can use prepared piña colada mix instead of the pineapple juice and cream of coconut. ■ *Yield: 4 drinks*

2 cups fresh or frozen strawberries
8 ounces light rum
12 ounces pineapple juice
4 ounces cream of coconut
4 ripe bananas, sliced
2 cups crushed ice

FOR THE GARNISH
pineapple wedges
orange slices
umbrella toothpicks

1 Mix the strawberries in a blender until they make a puree. Set aside and clean the blender.
2 Combine the rum, pineapple juice, cream of coconut, bananas, and ice in the blender.
3 Fill 4 large glasses less than halfway with the rum-pineapple mixture. Pour about ¼ cup strawberry puree. Alternate the rum-pineapple mixture with the strawberry puree. Take a knife and poke the mixture to help the red creep down, creating the "flow."
4 Garnish each drink with pineapple wedges, orange slices, and umbrella toothpicks.

HAWAIIAN PUNCH MAI TAIS

The original mai tais at our luau were so strong that the vapors alone were intoxicating. Our secret ingredient in this version—fruit punch—makes them a little less potent and a lot more tasty!
■ *Yield: 4 drinks*

2 ounces dark rum
2 ounces light rum
2 ounces curaçao
2 ounces apricot brandy
10 ounces Hawaiian Punch
(other fruit juices can be substituted)
ice cubes

FOR THE GARNISH
orange slices
pineapple wedges
umbrella toothpicks

1 Combine all ingredients except ice in a cocktail shaker and shake.
2 Pour into glasses filled with ice.
3 Garnish each drink with orange slices, pineapple wedges, and umbrella toothpicks.

BLACKBERRY-APPLE CREPES

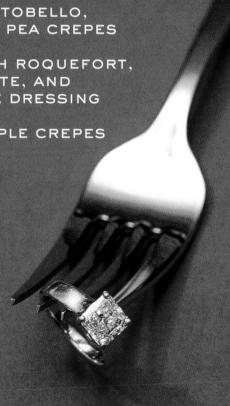

engagement crepe party

MENU

KIR ROYALES

SIMPLE CREPE BATTER

CRABMEAT McMUFFINS

RATATOUILLE

CHICKEN, PORTOBELLO,
AND SUGAR SNAP PEA CREPES

MIXED GREENS WITH ROQUEFORT,
POMEGRANATE, AND
ROSEMARY-LIME DRESSING

BLACKBERRY-APPLE CREPES

I DO DINNER

French crepes are our recipe for love

AGEWISE, WE'RE IN THE ZONE. It's that five-year window when it seems every coworker, neighbor, and person sitting next to you on the subway has just gotten engaged. Most Monday mornings, loud shrieks and giggles can be heard over cubicle walls as another "How did he ask?!" story gets told. Couples saunter ahead of you on the sidewalk hand-in-hand, making googly eyes at the windows of Tiffany's. No one saunters in New York! They could only be ring shopping. There are so many happy couples out there, it only follows that there are many happy celebrations in order.

We've all attended our share of engagement parties in the past. We've each cheerily chatted with Uncle Buster while watching our friend the Bride introduce the in-laws. We've met the saucy ladies from the Bridge Club; we've talked tuna casserole recipes; we know the drill. It's not that we don't love a good formal party, but as you can imagine, we feel the need to appropriate every occasion. So when Lucia became engaged one winter, we leaped on the opportunity to reinvent the ritual. In order to really distinguish ourselves, we also made it the one occasion for which the guest-of-honor would have to prepare a dish. After all, there's no free lunch in this cooking club, not even for the bride.

Because we couldn't think of anywhere more romantic than belle Paris, we decided to create a French feast. Katherine dreamily recalled a highlight of her recent trip to the city of love: long strolls along the Boulevard Saint-Germain with a warm Crepe Nutella in hand. It's like carrying around a little hazelnut security blanket. What could be more fabulous?

So in honor of things warm and sweet and indulgent, we decided we'd stuff everything in a crepe! (The decision really had nothing to do with the fact that Cynthia had just purchased a new crepe pan with a cute terrycloth-covered handle, we swear.) Becky, who was tempted to wrap her fillings in crepes *and* bacon, created a savory chicken dish for the main course. Lisa contributed a pepperless ratatouille to make sure that even at our love fest we all had our vegetables, and sensible Sharon figured we could all use some greens. And Bridey, who said she'd only pitch in if assigned dessert (oh, you know how they get), made an apple and blackberry filling that featured a tart little kick. To complement these luscious little bundles, Katherine tapped her mom for a decadent crabmeat hors d'oeuvre straight from New Orleans, which may have French roots of its own. This being French Night, however, we topped our salad with Roquefort because everyone knows France's way with cheese is simply . . . ooh-la-la! Finally, we anticipated many toasts to the bride and groom, so Cynthia suggested Kir Royales, elegant cocktails that proved a festive way to kick off the evening and the beginning of a lifetime. . . .

CREPE PREP

1. Don't leave the actual making of the crepes until the last minute—it's more time-consuming than you'd think. Prepare the crepes beforehand and keep them warm in an oven set at a low temperature. When your guests arrive, wouldn't you rather be playing hostess than standing over the stove all alone?

2. Unless, of course, you want to. If you're having a less formal shindig and you want to show off your new crepe pan, then by all means, invite the hordes into the kitchen! It can be fun to make crepes en masse—your guests will leave feeling not only sated and Frenchified, but also well versed in a newfound skill.

3. Get creative in your crepe construction. Try doing what we call the half-bowtie fold. Imagine the crepe as a circle equally divided by a set of perpendicular lines; put filling in one quadrant; fold the crepe in half, and then in half again. You'll have a triangular shape with one delicate, layered edge—*c'est très élégant.*

KIR ROYALES

Black currants, or cassis, have been used for medicinal purposes in France's Burgundy region for centuries. In its distilled state, the sweet liqueur has been used as a cure for snakebites, jaundice, and "wretchedness." A kir, made with white wine and crème de cassis, is named for Canon Felix Kir, a valiant leader of the French resistance during World War II (and future mayor of Dijon, the only region in the world whose climate yields black currants sweet enough to produce a drinkable crème de cassis). The kir's upscale cousin, the kir royale, is made with crème de cassis and champagne, and is guaranteed to eliminate even the slightest trace of wretchedness.
■ *Yield: 1 drink*

1 part crème de cassis
5 parts champagne
lemon peel

Pour crème de cassis into a champagne glass and then fill with champagne. Add peel.

SIMPLE CREPE BATTER

This easy batter can be used for both sweet and savory fillings, or, if you like, try adding more sugar or some cinnamon to the batter and *voilà!* You've got yourself a little French pancake—breakfast and dessert all in one. ■ *Yield: 20 crepes*

1 cup whole milk, at room temperature	**3 eggs**
⅓ cup water	**3 tablespoons unsalted butter, melted**
1 cup all-purpose flour	**1 teaspoon sugar**

I Mix all the ingredients in a blender until smooth. Transfer the mixture to a large mixing bowl; cover and chill in the refrigerator for 30 minutes. (The batter can be made the day before, too.)
2 Spray a nonstick pan with cooking spray and heat over medium heat. When the pan is hot, ladle in just enough batter to coat the bottom. Swirl around until the batter is as thin as possible.
3 Cook until the edges begin to brown, about 1 to 2 minutes. Carefully flip the crepe, and cook for another 30 seconds.
4 Repeat as often as necessary, remembering to add more cooking spray when needed. Keep the crepes warm in the oven at a low temperature until ready to serve.

BATTER UP: SHARON (LEFT) AND BECKY DO CREPE PREP FOR THE ENGAGEMENT PARTY

CRABMEAT McMUFFINS

Someday we'll tell Katherine that the real reason we wanted her in our club was because of her mother. Mrs. Fausset is a little firecracker of a lady who grew up in Houston, spent twelve years in Paris, and then settled in New Orleans—a culinary background anyone would envy. Katherine made these hors d'oeuvres for us once, and we all fell in love with them on the spot. The juvenile name is ours, but the recipe is all Kay Fausset, and it's as decadent and delicious as any Texan-Parisian-Louisianan infusion you can imagine. ▪ *Yield: 24 hors d'oeuvres*

6 ounces canned crabmeat
1 5.2-ounce package Boursin cheese
1½ tablespoons mayonnaise
½ tablespoon seasoned salt
½ tablespoon garlic salt or pressed fresh garlic
8 tablespoons (1 stick) unsalted butter, melted
6 English muffins, split and cut into quarters
chopped fresh parsley, for garnish

1 Preheat the oven to 400 degrees.
2 Mix all the ingredients except the English muffins and parsley in a large bowl; spread onto the English muffin quarters.
3 Place the muffins with spread on an ungreased cookie sheet, cover with aluminum foil, and put them in the freezer until you are ready to serve them, or for at least 10 minutes.
4 Uncover and cook for 10 to 15 minutes, until lightly browned.
5 Garnish with parsley.

RATATOUILLE

For our French vegetable dish, Lisa, who has a serious bell pepper aversion, decided to riff off the classic Provençal ragout and came up with this succulent version that includes not a single one. At our engagement party we wrapped it in a crepe, but ratatouille can be wonderful as a main course over couscous or rice, or try serving it cold as a summertime salad. ■ *Yield: 6 to 8 servings*

2 medium eggplants, peeled and diced into 1-inch cubes

salt

¼ cup extra-virgin olive oil

2 medium onions, chopped (about 2 cups)

7 plum tomatoes, seeded and chopped

2 zucchini, diced into 1-inch cubes

2 teaspoons tomato paste

2 teaspoons dried oregano

3 cloves garlic, minced

freshly ground pepper to taste

6 to 8 crepes (page 36)

1 Line a large colander with paper towels. Place the eggplant cubes in it, generously salt, and mix together.

2 In a large saucepan, heat the olive oil over medium heat. Add the onions and sauté until transparent, about 8 minutes.

3 Add the eggplant, tomatoes, zucchini, tomato paste, oregano, and garlic to the saucepan, and sauté for 15 minutes, stirring frequently.

4 Turn the heat to medium-low, cover, and simmer for about 35 minutes.

5 When the vegetable mixture is cooked through, season with salt and pepper.

6 Fill the crepes with the ratatouille and serve immediately.

"YOU MARRY ME, YOU MARRY MY COOKING CLUB." LUCIA FILLS PIETER IN ON THE DUTIES OF A CC HUSBAND.

CHICKEN, PORTOBELLO, AND SUGAR SNAP PEA CREPES

This is a wonderful savory filling that's a bit of a hybrid. The marinade used for the chicken and vegetables has an Asian influence (and is great for fish, by the way), but it's paired with a velouté sauce to give it a much richer, subtler taste. This sauce is one of the five "mother sauces" of French cuisine. Don't get intimidated by the fancy name; it's simply a white sauce made from a stock base and thickened with a white roux. It's great to have in your repertoire because it's an excellent base for other sauces, and you get the added bonus of using the term *mother sauce*.

■ *Yield: 4 to 6 servings*

FOR THE MARINADE
½ cup soy sauce
3 tablespoons fresh lime juice
1 tablespoon grated peeled fresh ginger
¼ cup extra-virgin olive oil
1 teaspoon freshly ground pepper

—

4 boneless, skinless chicken breasts
(about 1½ pounds), cooked and
cut into ½-inch-thick strips

4 portobello mushroom caps,
washed and cut into ¼-inch-thick strips
2 cups sugar snap peas

FOR THE VELOUTÉ SAUCE
3 tablespoons unsalted butter
3 tablespoons all-purpose flour
2 cups chicken stock
salt and freshly ground pepper to taste

—

4 to 6 crepes (page 36)

1   In a small bowl, combine all the marinade ingredients and stir vigorously until well blended.
2   In a large bowl, combine the chicken, mushroom caps, and snap peas.
3   Pour the marinade over the chicken mixture, mix thoroughly, and set aside.
4   To prepare the velouté sauce, in a large saucepan, melt the butter over medium-low heat.
5   Slowly whisk in the flour, stirring constantly for about 2 to 3 minutes, until the roux is smooth and just starts to bubble.
6   Whisk in the stock, ½ cup at a time, stirring constantly until smooth.
7   Bring the liquid to a boil, then reduce the heat to low and cook for about 10 more minutes. Season with salt and pepper, if desired. Set aside.
8   Strain the chicken mixture so it is free of extra marinade.
9   Pour the chicken mixture into the saucepan with the velouté sauce, and stir to mix well. Let simmer for about 5 more minutes, until the chicken and vegetables are heated through.
10 Fill the crepes with the chicken mixture and serve immediately.

engagement crepe party

MIXED GREENS WITH ROQUEFORT, POMEGRANATE, AND ROSEMARY-LIME DRESSING

This simple salad achieves a certain air of sophistication thanks to the addition of the Roquefort cheese. Dubbed by some "the king of cheeses," Roquefort was a favorite of Charlemagne's and is one of the oldest known cheeses in the world. We liked this "king of the cheese" label. It made us feel rather regal. And when the Roquefort is combined with the sweet-tart zing of the pomegranate seeds, it truly is a taste sensation. ■ *Yield: 4 to 6 servings*

FOR THE SALAD
6 cups mixed salad greens
¾ cup pomegranate kernels
1 Bosc pear, cored and sliced lengthwise into ½-inch wedges
½ cup crumbled Roquefort cheese (or other blue cheese)

FOR THE ROSEMARY-LIME DRESSING
3 tablespoons balsamic vinegar
3 tablespoons fresh lime juice
1 teaspoon sugar
**2 teaspoons chopped fresh rosemary,
or 1 teaspoon dried**
½ cup extra-virgin olive oil
salt and freshly ground pepper to taste

I   Combine the salad ingredients in a large bowl.

2   To prepare the dressing, whisk together the vinegar, lime juice, sugar, and rosemary. Slowly whisk in the olive oil until well mixed. Season with salt and pepper.

3   Right before serving, drizzle the dressing over the salad.

BLACKBERRY-APPLE CREPES

Less filling than apple pie and way more romantic, this dessert came about during our first Crepe Night that took place at one CC member's new pied-à-terre in Brooklyn. In honor of whirlwind romances, we came up with a dessert as exhilarating as new love . . . one little nibble, and we were all hooked. ■ *Yield: 6 to 8 servings*

2 tablespoons unsalted butter

**3 Golden Delicious apples, peeled, cored,
and sliced into ½-inch wedges**

¼ cup sugar

⅛ teaspoon salt

1 quart blackberries, cut in half lengthwise

¼ cup cognac

1 teaspoon grated lemon zest

1 pint whipped cream

—

6 to 8 crepes (page 36)

I Melt the butter in a large skillet over medium-low heat. Add the sliced apples and stir gently until warm and covered.

2 Pour in the sugar and salt. Continue to stir the contents gently, so the apples are evenly covered with sugar.

3 Reserve 6 to 8 blackberry halves for garnish, then add the rest to the apple mixture. Pour the cognac over the mixture, and sprinkle in the lemon zest. Gently stir the mixture, being careful not to break up any blackberries. Cover and let simmer on low heat for 3 to 4 minutes.

4 Spoon approximately ¼ cup filling per crepe.

5 Place a dollop of whipped cream on each crepe and top each with a fresh blackberry half. Serve immediately.

engagement crepe party

MEXICAN FLAG
ENCHILADAS, PICO
DE GALLO, AND
TORTILLA SOUP

mexican fiesta

MENU

Y TU MAMA'S TORTILLA SOUP

MEXICAN FLAG ENCHILADAS

SAUTÉED SHRIMP WITH
PAPAYA-HONEYDEW PICO DE GALLO

JICAMA, BLACK BEAN,
AND CORN SALAD

SOPAIPILLAS

MAKE-AHEAD MARGARITAS

TACO BELLES

We spice up Cinco de Mayo

OVER THE YEARS, our cooking club has celebrated the cuisines of many regions, and at times it's been hard to decide which one to choose. Switzerland? Slovenia? There are only so many Sundays a year. But there was never any doubt that come May 5, we would honor a certain south of the border country that we've always held close to our hearts. Not only did it give us the corn tortilla, but it is also responsible for the brilliant idea of putting cheese inside tortillas, rolling them up, smothering them with more cheese, and putting them in the oven until oozing and bubbly . . . ahh, Mexico. And so to pay homage to this lactose-tolerant region, we dusted off our serapes, set out the limes and salt, and had a frijoles-licious fiesta!

Cinco de Mayo celebrates Mexico's freedom and liberation from French invaders. Though not historically documented, we think this must be the reason for the popularity of the margarita; Becky can attest that after sucking down three, she indeed felt free as well as liberated. The menu for our fiesta includes a variety of authentic Mexican foods, yet they are all made with ingredients and spices you don't have to go to the far reaches of Oaxaca to find. We also feared that six courses of heavy Mexican food would likely make us feel more "oy vey" than "olé," so we came up with two delicious yet tummy-friendly dishes to round out the meal: Jicama, Black Bean, and Corn Salad and Sautéed Shrimp with Papaya-Honeydew Pico de Gallo.

Aside from the food, what is the real key to planning an unforgettable Cinco de Mayo party? We can't say it enough: piñata, piñata, piñata! If you think you're too old to put on a

blindfold yourself and swing wildly at a papier-mâché animal filled with candy, you're wrong. And if your last memory of what's inside includes stale peppermints and Smarties crushed into an inedible powder, don't worry. These days, you can custom-fill your piñata with whatever you want: Blow Pops and mini Butterfingers ("It's All About the Candy Piñata"), Godiva chocolates and flower petals ("Piñata Elegante"), even mini lipsticks and perfume samples ("The Lovely Lady")—basically, anything that can reasonably withstand a swinging bat and won't injure people when showering onto the ground. Lucia assured us that the Kit Kat bar shot at high velocity into the side of her head was worth the temporary pain. Be creative with your piñata stuffing, but be forewarned: If the spoils that come pouring out from the final, glorious blow turn out to be something disappointing like mini deodorants or little boxes of raisins, you're going to find yourself faced with a mob of angry people armed with a large bat.

FOR A FANTASTIC FIESTA

1. MUSIC: There's something about mariachi music that simply makes people happy. Recommended CDs: anything by Vicente Fernández and Los Lobos' *La Pistola y El Corazón.*

2. PREPARE YOUR MARGARITAS AHEAD OF TIME: (See our Make-Ahead Margaritas recipe, page 55.) Remember how in *Return of the Jedi* Princess Leia is chained up in a gold bikini to Jabba the Hutt? Well, that's exactly what it will feel like if you're stuck chained to your blender all night having to fill margarita orders for your guests. Instead, make and freeze multiple batches in advance.

3. DECORATIONS: We held our first annual Mexican fiesta in Lisa's former tiny apartment. When we walked in to see that she had strung up a piñata in her shoebox-size living room, where it was undoubtedly going to cause some wall damage, we were touched that she would go to such lengths for our amusement. And it was one of the best Cooking Clubs we can recall. One especially memorable highlight: watching a pregnant Sharon going to town with the piñata bat.

Y TU MAMA'S TORTILLA SOUP

This soup must have been someone's mama's recipe, because it's like eating a warm hug in a bowl. The garlicky broth is ladled over slices of tender chicken, then topped with shredded cheese, fresh cilantro, and strips of fried corn tortillas. But if you're tempted to use store-bought tortilla chips instead of frying your own, think again. After all, the point is to celebrate Mexico, not insult it. So save the bag of Tostitos for your Super Bowl party and fry up your own for this delicious and hearty soup. ■ *Yield: 6 appetizer servings*

1 pound boneless, skinless chicken breasts, rinsed and patted dry with paper towels

2 to 3 cups vegetable oil for frying

6 6-inch corn tortillas, cut into ¼-inch strips

2 tablespoons extra-virgin olive oil

2 tablespoons unsalted butter

1 whole head garlic, finely minced

1 large onion, finely chopped

2 teaspoons cumin

3 teaspoons chili powder

1 14½-ounce can diced tomatoes

6 cups chicken broth

1 egg, beaten

¾ cup shredded Monterey Jack cheese

¾ cup shredded cheddar cheese

fresh cilantro, chopped

1 Bring a medium pot of water to a boil. Poach the chicken breasts until cooked through, about 15 minutes. Remove from water. When cool enough to handle, cut into strips and set aside.

2 Heat 1 inch of oil over medium-high heat in a large skillet. In batches of four, fry the tortilla strips for about 30 seconds, until crisp. Remove with a slotted spoon, drain on paper towels, and set aside.

3 Heat the olive oil and melt the butter in a large soup pot over medium heat. Add the garlic and onion. Sauté until the onion is translucent, then add the cumin and chili powder. Sauté an additional minute, then add the tomatoes. Let simmer for about 5 minutes, stirring occasionally. Add the chicken broth; bring to a boil. Reduce the heat to medium-low and cook, uncovered, for 20 minutes. Briskly whisk in the egg.

4 Ladle the soup into individual bowls. Garnish with the chicken strips, fried tortilla strips, cheese, and cilantro.

TWO HOT TAMALES, LUCIA AND SHARON, COME PREPARED FOR THE CINCO DE MAYO FIESTA

MEXICAN FLAG ENCHILADAS

These enchiladas, which are resplendent with the colors of the Mexican flag (red, white, and green), are the show-pony of the meal. For added effect, put the sour cream in a plastic bag, poke a hole in the bottom, and squirt zigzags over the top. ■ *Yield: 6 servings*

FOR THE SAUCE

1 tablespoon vegetable oil

4 cloves garlic, minced

2 14½-ounce cans diced tomatoes

¼ cup tomato paste

½ cup water

1 tablespoon finely chopped jalapeño chiles

¾ cup chopped scallions (white parts plus 2 inches of green)

¾ cup canned green chiles

½ cup chopped fresh cilantro

1 teaspoon salt

¼ teaspoon freshly ground pepper

FOR THE FILLING

2 tablespoons vegetable oil

2 cups chopped onions

1 pound fresh spinach, destemmed and chopped

2 cups grated Monterey Jack cheese

2 cups grated mozzarella cheese

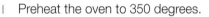

12 6-inch corn tortillas

FOR THE GARNISH

1 cup sour cream

¾ cup seeded and chopped tomatoes

¾ cup chopped scallions (green parts only)

1 Preheat the oven to 350 degrees.

2 To make the sauce, heat the oil in a saucepan over medium-high heat. Add the garlic and sauté for 2 minutes. Stir in the tomatoes, tomato paste, and water. Bring to a boil. Cover, reduce the heat and let simmer for 10 minutes. Remove from the heat and transfer to a blender or food processor. Add the remaining sauce ingredients and puree until blended. Pour 1½ cups of the sauce into a 9-by-13-inch baking dish. Reserve the remaining sauce and set aside.

3 To make the filling, heat the oil in a large sauté pan over medium heat. Sauté the onions just until soft. Add the spinach and cook, covered, until the spinach is wilted; set aside.

4 Place 6 tortillas between damp paper towels and microwave for 45 seconds to soften. Then place 1 tablespoon of the spinach mixture down the middle of each tortilla. Top each with 1 to 2 tablespoons of mixed cheeses. Roll the tortillas and place seam side down in the sauce-covered baking dish. Heat up the second batch of tortillas and repeat.

5 Spoon the reserved sauce on top of the tortillas, and cover with the remaining cheese mixture. Bake for 25 minutes. Top with sour cream, chopped tomatoes, and scallions, and serve.

SAUTÉED SHRIMP WITH PAPAYA-HONEYDEW PICO DE GALLO

We wanted to think "outside the taco" for this menu, and we're pretty sure you can't find this dish at the Bell. The spicy shrimp melds wonderfully with the sweet fruit in the pico de gallo. It even spurred a lengthy Cooking Club debate on why is there hype about the burrito when you could eat this. We served these shrimp along with dinner, but if you want to make it into a stand-alone first course, fry strips of corn tortillas in oil, sprinkle with kosher salt, and serve individual portions of pico de gallo and shrimp on beds of the fried tortillas. Or, serve this with warm corn tortillas for soft tacos. ■ *Yield: 6 servings*

FOR THE PICO DE GALLO
2 cups diced papaya
2 cups diced honeydew melon
2 avocados, diced
1 jalapeño chile, seeded and finely chopped
1 cup diced onion
2 to 3 tablespoons fresh lemon juice
2 tablespoons fresh lime juice
salt and freshly ground pepper to taste

3 tablespoons extra-virgin olive oil
4 cloves garlic, pressed
1½ teaspoons cumin
2 teaspoons chili powder
½ teaspoon salt
¼ teaspoon freshly ground pepper
2 pounds medium shrimp, peeled and deveined

mexican fiesta

1 Combine the pico de gallo ingredients in a medium bowl. Refrigerate, covered, until ready to serve. Allow to return to room temperature before serving.

2 Heat the olive oil in a large skillet over medium heat. Add the garlic and sauté for 30 seconds. (Do not let brown.) Add the cumin and chili powder and sauté an additional 2 minutes. Add the shrimp, stirring often, and cook it until it is just pink; be careful not to overcook it. Remove from heat and add salt and pepper. Serve immediately on top of individual servings of pico de gallo.

MORE, POR FAVOR:
CYNTHIA SERVES KATHERINE
SOME JICAMA, BLACK BEAN,
AND CORN SALAD

JICAMA, BLACK BEAN, AND CORN SALAD

Sharon, of course, was responsible for this healthy Mexican dish. And, no, that's not an oxymoron. The beauty of this salad is that you could serve it to hungry vaqueros at the Circle Q ranch, as well as to stair-stepping socialites at the Canyon Ranch. Even Sharon's husband said that if given a choice, he'd choose this salad over his beloved triple-decker corned beef sandwiches. Basically, you'll be hard-pressed to find anyone who won't like this combination of crunchy jicama, black beans, and sweet corn, with the zing of the fresh lime juice. ■ *Yield: 6 servings*

1 cup peeled and diced jicama

1 15-ounce can black beans, drained and rinsed

1 cup thawed frozen sweet corn

1 red bell pepper, seeded and diced

1 small red onion, finely chopped

½ cup chopped fresh flat-leaf parsley

¼ cup fresh lime juice

1 tablespoon extra-virgin olive oil

1 heaping teaspoon cumin

1 heaping teaspoon chili powder

salt and freshly ground pepper to taste

1   Combine the jicama, beans, corn, pepper, onion, and parsley in a large bowl.

2   In a separate bowl, whisk together the lime juice, olive oil, cumin, and chili powder. Add to the salad and mix thoroughly. Season with salt and pepper.

SOPAIPILLAS

When Becky told us she was going to make sopaipillas for our Mexican fiesta, we got jealous: Why should one person alone have the joy of making fried dough? So Becky graciously set us loose in her spacious SoHo kitchen so we could all get in on the action. (She also advised her husband, Steve, to go out for Poker Night. Six women in a kitchen with unrestricted access to fried dough had the possibility of turning into a scene that no man should see.) We decided the only part better than watching squares of dough puff up into delightful little golden pillows was drizzling them with cinnamon and honey, then popping them into our mouths. ▪ *Yield: about 36 sopaipillas*

4 cups all-purpose flour
4 teaspoons baking powder
1 teaspoon salt
1 tablespoon shortening
1 egg, beaten
1 cup cold water
1 cup honey
½ teaspoon cinnamon
vegetable oil for frying

1   Combine the flour, baking powder, and salt in a large bowl. Cut in the shortening. Knead in the egg and water to form a stiff dough.
2   Roll out the dough into a ¼-inch-thick layer. Cut into squares or diamond shapes, about 2 by 2 inches.
3   In a small bowl, stir the honey and cinnamon together. Set aside.
4   Heat the oil in a deep skillet (about 2 inches deep). The oil should be *very* hot. Fry the sopaipillas in small batches. As they begin to puff up, turn them over in the oil. When the second sides have puffed, remove and drain on paper towels. Serve while still warm with the honey-cinnamon sauce.

MAKE-AHEAD MARGARITAS

Katherine's two aunts from Houston, Aunt Isla and Aunt Patricia, each claim this margarita recipe as their own. Rather than have this festive beverage become the cause of a family feud, Katherine decided to credit them both. And there is a reason why both take such pride in these margaritas— they are fantastic. Refills require only a quick trip to the freezer instead of a messy bout with the blender. And the fresh lime juice gives them zing. ■ *Serves 6 to 8*

4 cups tequila
1 cup triple sec
¼ cup fresh lime juice
6 ounces canned frozen lemonade, thawed
6 ounces canned frozen limeade, thawed
4 cups water

Mix all the ingredients. Transfer to plastic containers or large plastic freezer bags. Store, covered, in the freezer for at least 24 hours, stirring several times during that time. To serve, remove from the freezer, stir, and pour into margarita glasses.

mexican fiesta

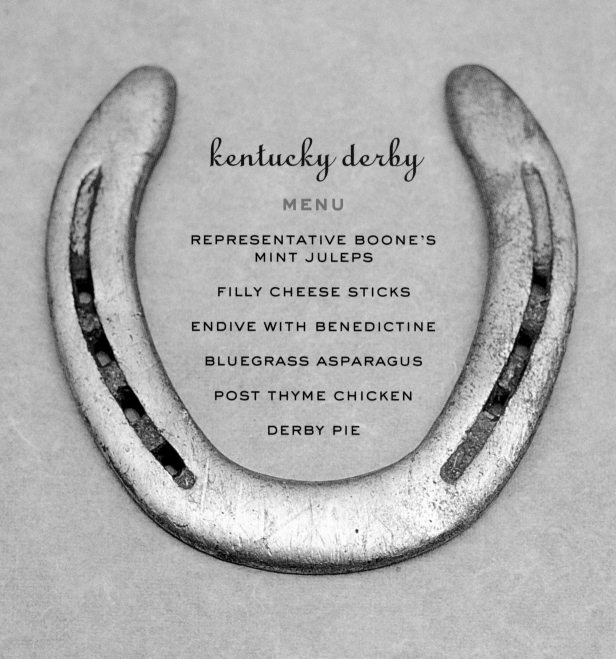

kentucky derby

MENU

**REPRESENTATIVE BOONE'S
MINT JULEPS**

FILLY CHEESE STICKS

ENDIVE WITH BENEDICTINE

BLUEGRASS ASPARAGUS

POST THYME CHICKEN

DERBY PIE

JOCKEY FOR HER

Hats off to our fastest Derby Day menu

IT'S SAID THAT THE Kentucky Derby is the most exciting two minutes in sports: Thorough-bred horses worth their weight in gold thunder around the Churchill Downs track, leaving only a streak of the jockeys' brightly colored silks in their wake. That the "Run for the Roses," as the Derby is known (the winning horse is draped in a wreath of red roses), lasts for a mere two minutes doesn't seem to bother Kentuckians, who spend the three weeks preceding it in an anticipatory whirlwind of parties, parades, and fireworks, not to mention hot-air balloon and steamboat races.

Even if you have only one day to celebrate, it's well worth making the most of this first leg of the Triple Crown. Unless you live in Kentucky or will be visiting Louisville (in which case you probably have firm views, as well as ancestral traditions, about how the day should be celebrated), we'll assume that you'll be watching the event on TV. But unlike your average Super Bowl party, which runs 2-to-1 odds of being commandeered by a dictatorial host who insists on a no-talking policy, the TV takes a subordinate role in Derby entertain-ing. In fact, last year we spent most of that first Saturday in May—when the race is always held—out of earshot of the TV, in our friend Alexandra's backyard.

In honor of the lightning speed at which the thoroughbreds bolt around the track, we decided that Derby Night would feature fast versions of signature Kentucky dishes—to allow more time for CC members to find a suitable hat (an essential accessory), to handicap the race, or to make a pit stop at one of New York's scenic off-track-betting shops. This ruled out a few classics, such as beaten biscuits, traditionally made by stirring the dough with a wooden mallet or axe for more than a half hour, and Kentucky burgoo, a stew that usually boasts about thirty ingredients, including rabbit, mutton, veal, ham, and chicken. Instead, we've focused on universal crowd pleasers and added bourbon whenever possible. (Our bourbon of choice would have to be ten-year, 90-proof Old Rip Van Winkle, as the distillery was founded by Julian "Pappy" Van Winkle, our friend Louisa's great-grandfather.)

Whether given by frat boys or ladies who lunch, any self-respecting Derby party must include mint juleps, preferably served in frosted silver cups. We borrowed some from Katherine's mother, who received no fewer than fifteen when she was married. Of course, if you don't have silver mint julep cups (or access to a generous Southern mother), there are other options. Collectible Derby glasses imprinted with every horse that's ever won are issued each year and can be purchased (along with paper and plastic party products that sport the Derby logo) at www.exclusivelyequine.com and www.racingmuseum.org. Also available are win-place-show tickets for your in-house betting needs, as well as canvas belts embroidered with racehorses and even toilet paper emblazoned with a horse motif. Regardless of how you celebrate the Derby—with a few friends or a few hundred—taking part in the sport of kings is guaranteed to make you feel like a queen.

kentucky derby

DERBY DO'S

1. HAVE RED ROSES:
While the garden party set often arrange their Derby roses in a floral horseshoe, placing them in a vase is just fine. (Particularly if it's one engraved with a horse!)

2. TELL EVERYONE TO WEAR A HAT: There's nothing that lets you channel your inner Southern belle like wearing an outsize hat, preferably one in a pastel or white organza.

3. PLAY THE PONIES:
Write each horse's name on a piece of paper. Then have everyone draw one of the names out of a hat and put five dollars in the purse for the winning "owner."

REPRESENTATIVE BOONE'S MINT JULEPS

This recipe came to us by way of our friend Elizabeth's dad, Joe Graves, who served as both a Kentucky state senator and a state representative. While in the House in 1972, his fellow representative George Street Boone shared this recipe with him. This is an adapted version (the original has nineteen steps!), but we've tried to retain the essence of this impressive drink.
■ *Yield: 6 drinks*

2 bunches mint (about 2 cups); one rinsed with water,
the other left unwashed
12 ounces bourbon, refrigerated
2 tablespoons honey
crushed ice (about 5 cups),
kept in the freezer until ready to use
1 tablespoon powdered sugar

1 Remove the leaves from the washed mint and place them in a large bowl. Add the bourbon and honey. Using the back of a wooden spoon or a pestle, crush the liquid-covered mint. (If time permits, let this steep for a few hours, but it's not necessary.)

2 Place about ¼ cup crushed ice in each cup. Divide the honey mixture evenly among the cups, then fill the remaining space in the cups with crushed ice.

3 Place the unwashed mint and the powdered sugar in a paper or plastic bag and shake vigorously, to coat the mint. (This doesn't work if the mint is wet.) Garnish each drink with 4 sprigs of the sugar-coated mint.

KATHERINE, BECKY,
AND JIM (BEAM)
SHARE MINT JULEPS

FILLY CHEESE STICKS

Those ubiquitous crunchy store-bought cheese twists are tasty, but inevitably it seems that after the first funny joke at a party, someone needs the Heimlich maneuver after inhaling one. These softer cheese sticks are the oldest trick in the book: The pastry is store-bought, but the end product tastes fantastically homemade. Plus, it isn't a choking hazard. ▪ *Yield: 40 cheese sticks*

½ teaspoon salt
1 teaspoon paprika
1 teaspoon cayenne pepper
1 sheet frozen puff pastry
(about 9 inches by 9 inches), thawed
½ cup finely grated sharp cheddar cheese

1   Preheat the oven to 375 degrees.
2   In a small bowl, mix together the salt, paprika, and cayenne pepper. Spread this mixture onto a clean surface on which you will be rolling out the dough.
3   Place the dough on the dusted surface, sprinkle the cheese on top, and roll out the dough until it is a rectangle that measures roughly 10 by 13 inches and is about ⅛ inch thick.
4   Slice the dough in half lengthwise (so that you are cutting parallel to the longer side of the rectangle). Then slice each half into ½-inch strips (so you're now cutting parallel to the *shorter* side of the rectangle).
5   Holding each strip by the ends, twist the dough a few times before placing on an ungreased cookie sheet (lined with parchment paper, if desired). Cook for about 7 to 8 minutes, until the twists are golden. Serve the same day.

AT RISK OF BEING CONFUSED WITH A GARDEN CLUB, THE COOKING CLUB GETS DECKED OUT FOR THE DERBY

ENDIVE WITH BENEDICTINE

We've been told that this spread was made famous at the turn of the century (the *other* turn of the century) by a Louisville caterer named Jenny Benedict. It's traditionally made with cream cheese, onion, and cucumber, and then tinted with green food coloring. Since Lucia never misses an opportunity to use goat cheese, she's updated the recipe. ▪ *Yield: 8 servings*

3 tablespoons peeled, seeded, and grated cucumber
1½ tablespoons chopped fresh chives, plus extra for garnish
¾ cup fresh goat cheese (about 6 ounces)
freshly ground pepper to taste
3 heads endive, separated into individual leaves

1 Place the cucumber between several paper towels and squeeze to remove excess liquid.
2 Using a food processor or an electric mixer, blend together the cucumber, chives, and goat cheese. Season with pepper.
3 Place a dollop of spread on the base of each endive leave. Garnish with chives.

BLUEGRASS ASPARAGUS

Kitty Terry, a true Kentucky lady, told us that it's traditional to serve asparagus at a Derby party because that's always been the freshest vegetable in season in May, when the race is held. Of course, once you taste these, you won't want to wait a year for them. ▪ *Yield: 6 to 8 servings*

2 bunches asparagus, bottoms trimmed
large bowl of ice water
½ cup extra-virgin olive oil

3 tablespoons fresh lemon juice
1 teaspoon poppy seeds
¼ teaspoon salt

1 Bring a large pot of salted water to a boil. Once the water is boiling, add the asparagus and cook for 3 minutes.
2 When the asparagus are crisp-tender, remove from the heat, drain in a colander, and immediately immerse in ice water to stop the cooking. When the asparagus have cooled, drain and arrange on a serving platter.
3 In a small bowl, whisk together the olive oil, lemon juice, poppy seeds, and salt. Pour the dressing over the asparagus and serve.

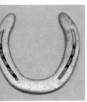

POST THYME CHICKEN

Because our friend Jess Boer's dad hails from Kentucky, we decided that her easy herbed chicken qualified for a Derby Night dinner. We served it with a salad topped with fried tomatoes and a side of Bluegrass Asparagus, all of which can be prepared faster than you can say "Fusaichi Pegasus."

■ *Yield: 4 to 6 servings*

1 cup finely grated fresh Parmesan cheese
1 cup bread crumbs
¼ cup minced fresh thyme (hard stems removed)
2 eggs
6 boneless, skinless, thin-sliced chicken breasts
(about 2 pounds), rinsed and patted dry with paper towels
(pounded to ½-inch thickness if necessary)
salt and freshly ground pepper to taste

1　Preheat the broiler, placing the oven rack directly under it.

2　In a large bowl, combine the cheese, bread crumbs, and thyme. In a medium bowl, whisk the eggs until combined.

3　Season the chicken breasts with salt and pepper. One by one, dip each breast into the egg, then into the bread-crumb mixture to coat. Place the chicken on a nonstick cookie sheet and cook it directly under the broiler for about 2 minutes on each side until it is golden brown and cooked through.

kentucky derby

DERBY PIE

According to the website A Taste of Kentucky, the original Derby Pie recipe (a patented trade secret) must be credited to George Kern, who was the manager of the restaurant at the Melrose Inn in Prospect, Kentucky. (You can buy an original one at www.atasteofkentucky.com.) We've spotted several imitations, all of which appear to be in the pecan pie family. Our version includes chocolate and bourbon, additions that we couldn't resist. (Note: If you have five extra minutes, use the other piecrust in the package to cut out shapes and decorate the top. Cynthia created leaves, but a horseshoe would be a no-brainer.) ■ *Yield: 8 to 10 servings*

4 tablespoons (½ stick) unsalted butter, softened
1 cup firmly packed light brown sugar
3 eggs
½ cup light corn syrup
2 tablespoons bourbon
¼ teaspoon salt
1½ cups chopped pecans
¼ cup mini chocolate chips
1 Pillsbury refrigerated 9-inch piecrust
pecan halves (optional)
vanilla ice cream or whipped cream (optional)

1 Preheat the oven to 350 degrees. Place a cookie sheet in the oven.

2 In a large bowl, beat together the butter and sugar. Beat in the eggs, corn syrup, bourbon, and salt. Stir in the pecans and chocolate chips.

3 Line a 9-inch pie dish (or a 10-inch tart pan) with the crust. (**NOTE:** If you use a tart pan, fill the pan two-thirds of the way and discard the rest of the batter.) Pour in the pecan mixture. If desired, top with pecan halves or other decorations. Place the pie on the cookie sheet in the oven and bake for 40 to 45 minutes, until the top of the pie is firm to the touch. Serve with ice cream or whipped cream if desired.

kentucky derby

LEMON BABY CAKES

baby shower tea

MENU

**CURRIED EGG SALAD
TEA SANDWICHES**

**SMOKED SALMON, CUCUMBER,
AND MASCARPONE TEA SANDWICHES**

B-L-TEAS

MINI MAPLE SCONES

**WHITE CHOCOLATE–DIPPED
STRAWBERRIES WITH HAZELNUTS**

LEMON BABY CAKES

TEA FOR TWO

A proper party for our mom-to-be

WHEN SHARON ANNOUNCED that she had a bun in the oven (not of the sticky or hot-cross variety), we knew a celebratory baby shower was in order. Cynthia quickly proposed an afternoon tea to ring in the next generation of Cooking Club, but our initial response was as strong as watered-down Earl Grey—there were several disappointed groans, and Becky grimly asked if we'd have to wear bonnets. But Katherine nobly rallied to Chef Cyn's defense: Sure, a tea did evoke images of blue-haired ladies in white gloves, but it's still fit for the Queen. And doesn't every new mom deserve a little royal treatment before her life is overtaken by diaper genies and drool?

Suddenly, our closet tea lovers emerged: Lucia sheepishly admitted her penchant for sandwiches with the crusts cut off. Lisa confessed to a former English Breakfast addiction. And everyone agreed that dainty cucumber sandwiches and bite-size cakes seemed in keeping with cute little sippy cups, teddy bear socks, and those irresistible mini Nike sneakers with the Velcro straps. And who says teatime has to be dull? Underwater tea parties were always fun, albeit brief. And who could forget *Alice in Wonderland*—now *that* was a tea party! We're not quite sure what the Mad Hatter was slipping into his pot, but we stuck to classic lemon, milk, and sugar as our condiments and even included an herbal option for those looking to kick the caffeine habit.

Lisa, who has watched the BBC version of *Pride and Prejudice* a few more times than can be considered normal, offered to do a slo-mo viewing to see exactly how Colin Firth butters his muffin. And Katherine agreed to hit up a few Southern belles from her hometown of New Orleans for advice. The rest of us sought out snooty Anglophiles, Manhattan tea salons, and the World Wide Web to see what we could soak up. We soon learned that, in England, high tea originated as a working-class meal to stave off late afternoon hunger until dinner. That sounded a lot like working girls we know, who make late afternoon jaunts to the office vending machine to, well, stave off hunger until dinner. But M&M's and pretzel rods apparently do not count as appropriate teatime fare, though they do fit the rule that tea food must fit between the thumb and forefinger. We decided to forgo the English rules of "napkin etiquette," but we embraced the structure of three courses that go in order from savory sandwiches, to scones, to sweet cakes. Having a tea also allowed us to make everything in advance (save boiling the water), which left more time to practice baby talk with our newly acquired British accents.

TIPS FOR BREWING THE PERFECT CUPPA

For proper technique, we asked an Englishwoman, of course. Our friend Jean says her number one complaint with American tea is that it's never served hot enough, perhaps due to the dearth of tea cozies this side of the Atlantic. To begin, she says, heat a kettle of cold springwater on the stove. When the water comes to a rolling boil, pour a little of the water into the teapot, swirl around to warm up the china, then pour the water out into the sink. Add one teaspoonful of loose tea for each person, plus "one for the pot." Then pour in the boiled water and let it steep for three to four minutes. Add sugar, if desired, to your cup, then the milk (most English take their tea light) and pour the tea through a handheld strainer to keep loose leaves from going into the cup. Tea bags are OK, as long as they are hidden discreetly in the pot—never the cup or saucer! Be sure to drink tea right away or remove the tea bags, as oversteeped tea tastes bitter.

baby shower tea

CURRIED EGG SALAD TEA SANDWICHES

Tipping a bowler hat to a former British colony, this egg salad is subtly exotic thanks to Indian curry and sweet currants. ■ *Yield: 12 sandwiches*

12 slices Pepperidge Farm thin-sliced white bread,*
or thin-sliced pumpernickel bread
4 hard-boiled eggs
4 tablespoons mayonnaise
1½ teaspoons curry powder
¼ teaspoon paprika
salt to taste
2 tablespoons currants

1 Cut the crusts off the bread to make each slice a perfect square. We find that by stacking half the slices and using a very sharp knife, you can cut the crusts off a bunch of slices at the same time.

2 Remove the shells from the eggs. Cut each egg in half, place the yolks in a medium bowl, and set the whites aside. To the yolks, add the mayonnaise, curry powder, paprika, and salt, and, with a fork, mash the yolks and combine all the ingredients. Mince the egg whites; add to the yolk mixture and stir until well combined. Stir in the currants.

3 Spread approximately 2 tablespoonfuls of egg salad on 1 slice of bread, top with 1 plain slice of bread, and slice diagonally (or into quarters, if using larger bread). Continue with all the remaining slices of bread.

NOTE: If you are not planning to serve the sandwiches right away, we recommend not slicing them ahead of time. Instead, stack them, covered with a slightly damp cloth, then slice them right before you are ready to serve. Otherwise, the edges of the bread will become dry.

✳ A NOTE ON BREAD FOR TEA SANDWICHES: We found that Pepperidge Farm thin-sliced white bread was the perfect consistency and taste for our tea sandwiches, as well as the perfect size. Each slice, halved diagonally, makes one sandwich. Larger bread will work fine; you may just have to quarter each slice diagonally, giving you four slices, rather than two. Day-old bread works great, and cookie cutters can be used to cut pretty shapes out of the bread.

DON'T LET THE SANDWICH SIZE FOOL YOU. AT SHARON'S SHOWER, WE WERE ALL EATING FOR TWO.

SMOKED SALMON, CUCUMBER, AND MASCARPONE TEA SANDWICHES

Mascarpone is a soft Italian cheese that you may know as one of the primary ingredients in tiramisù. But in this savory sandwich, its irresistibly buttery flavor complements two more classic tea sandwich ingredients. ▪ *Yield: 12 sandwiches*

12 slices Pepperidge Farm thin-sliced white bread
½ small cucumber
4 ounces smoked salmon
¼ cup mascarpone cheese

1 Cut the crusts off the bread to make each slice a perfect square. We find that by stacking half the slices and using a very sharp knife you can cut the crusts off a bunch of slices at the same time.

2 Peel, halve, and seed the cucumber. Cut into very thin slices.

3 Cut the salmon into small rectangular pieces (about 2-by-1-inch slices).

4 Spread a thin layer of mascarpone cheese on 1 slice of bread; layer a couple of slices of salmon and cucumber. Top with 1 plain slice of bread, and slice diagonally (or into quarters, if using larger bread). Continue with all the remaining slices of bread.

NOTE: If you are not planning to serve the sandwiches right away, we recommend not slicing them ahead of time. Instead, stack them, covered with a slightly damp cloth, then slice them right before you are ready to serve. Otherwise, the edges of the bread will become dry.

❉ See the footnote on page 72.

All-American, yes. However, we just couldn't resist making a bite-size take on the club-size classic. One taste and we think even the Earl of Sandwich would approve. ▪ *Yield: 12 sandwiches*

12 slices Pepperidge Farm thin-sliced white bread
2 tablespoons mayonnaise
10 slices cooked bacon, crumbled
2 small tomatoes, halved, seeded, and thinly sliced
½ cup baby greens

I   Cut the crusts off the bread to make each slice a perfect square. We find that by stacking half the slices and using a very sharp knife you can cut the crusts off a bunch of slices at the same time.

2   Spread a thin layer of mayonnaise on half the slices of bread; layer the crumbled bacon, tomato slices, and baby greens. Top with the remaining bread halves, and slice diagonally (or into quarters, if using larger bread).

N O T E : If you are not planning to serve the sandwiches right away, we recommend not slicing them ahead of time. Instead, stack them, covered with a slightly damp cloth, then slice them right before you are ready to serve. Otherwise, the edges of the bread will become dry.

❊ See the footnote on page 72.

baby shower tea

MINI MAPLE SCONES

Cynthia's parents live in Vermont, and she often returns from holidays with enough maple syrup for a year's worth of brunch nights. Taking advice from her mom, she subscribed to the Green Mountain adage that maple makes anything taste better. In England, scones are traditionally served with clotted cream and preserves. We considered making our own clotted cream, until we realized that it entails leaving unpasteurized milk to sit out for about twelve hours, unrefrigerated. So unless you have a cow in your backyard, and a strong stomach, try a jar of the imported kind found in some gourmet markets. ■ *Yield: about 2 dozen scones*

12 tablespoons (1½ sticks) unsalted butter

3 cups all-purpose flour

⅓ cup firmly packed light brown sugar

½ teaspoon salt

4 teaspoons baking powder

1 egg

½ cup heavy cream

½ teaspoon vanilla extract

1 teaspoon maple flavoring

⅓ cup plus a few extra tablespoons maple syrup

1 cup coarsely chopped pecans or walnuts

1   Cut the butter into tablespoon-size pieces and place in the freezer for at least 20 minutes.

2   Preheat the oven to 400 degrees. Adjust the oven rack to the middle level. Line a cookie sheet with parchment paper; set aside.

3   In a food processor, combine the flour, sugar, salt, and baking powder. Process until the ingredients are well blended. Add the frozen butter pieces and pulse on low until the mixture resembles coarse meal. Transfer the mixture to a large bowl.

4   In a medium bowl, beat the egg until foamy; add the cream. Beat for a few more strokes, then add the vanilla extract, maple flavoring, and ⅓ cup maple syrup; beat until just combined.

5   Make a well in the center of the dry ingredients and pour the liquid mixture into it. Fold the flour mixture into the liquid until just combined. Fold in the nuts.

6   Wash, dry, and flour your hands, then turn the dough onto a lightly floured surface and knead just enough to form into a ball. Either roll or pat the dough, using the heel of your hand, to make a ¾-inch-thick circle. Using a lightly floured, fluted cookie cutter, cut the dough into the desired shapes. If you have trouble removing the dough from the cookie cutter, use the pointed end of a paring knife to loosen the dough from the cutter. Place the scones about 1 inch apart on the lined cookie sheet. Brush the top of each scone with maple syrup. Bake for 10 to 12 minutes, or until lightly browned.

WHITE CHOCOLATE–DIPPED STRAWBERRIES WITH HAZELNUTS

Chocolate-covered strawberries are always a special treat, but they're surprisingly easy to make. You can substitute dark chocolate as well as experiment with different coatings, such as shredded coconut or rainbow sprinkles. ▪ *Yield: 2 dozen strawberries*

24 large ripe strawberries
½ cup hazelnuts
**8 ounces good-quality white chocolate,
broken into small chunks**

1 Line a cookie sheet with waxed or parchment paper; set aside.

2 Wash the strawberries, leaving the stems intact, and gently dry with paper towels.

3 In a food processor, process the hazelnuts for about 10 seconds, until chopped well (there will be some finer dust as well as chopped pieces). Pour into a bowl and set aside.

4 In a double boiler over low heat, melt the chocolate, stirring as needed until all lumps disappear. (Make sure that the inside of the melting pot is clean and completely dry when you start.)

5 Holding a strawberry by the stem, dip about three quarters of the way into the chocolate, then roll in the chopped hazelnuts and place on the lined cookie sheet. Refrigerate the strawberries until completely cooled and chocolate is hardened, at least 20 minutes.

baby shower tea

LEMON BABY CAKES

In honor of the baby boy- or girl-to-be, we baked these lemon yogurt cupcakes in mini muffin tins. We tinted the lemon cream cheese frosting pale pink and blue for the shower theme, but feel free to leave them au naturel, or use regular-size muffin tins for a party celebrating adult-size boys and girls. ▪ *Yield: 3 dozen mini-cupcakes, 1½ dozen regular cupcakes*

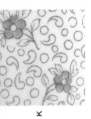

FOR THE CAKE

2¼ cups cake flour
½ teaspoon baking soda
1 teaspoon baking powder
½ teaspoon salt
8 tablespoons (1 stick) unsalted butter
1 cup sugar
1 egg plus 2 egg whites
1 teaspoon vanilla extract
1 teaspoon lemon extract
2 tablespoons lemon zest
1 cup plain yogurt

FOR THE FROSTING

5 tablespoons unsalted butter, softened
3 ounces cream cheese, softened
½ teaspoon vanilla extract
3 tablespoons fresh lemon juice
4 cups powdered sugar
food coloring (optional)
sprinkles (optional)

I   Have all ingredients at room temperature. Preheat the oven to 350 degrees. Line mini muffin tins with paper liners; set aside.

2   In a medium bowl, sift together the flour, baking soda, baking powder, and salt; set aside.

3   In a large bowl, using an electric mixer, beat the butter until creamy, about 30 seconds. Gradually add the sugar and beat on high speed about 3 to 5 minutes, until pale and light.

4   Beat in the egg and whites, one at a time. Add the vanilla extract, lemon extract, and zest and beat on low speed until combined.

5   Add the flour mixture in thirds, alternating with half the yogurt at a time, and beat on low speed, scraping the sides of the bowl with a rubber spatula as needed, until well blended.

6   Pour the batter into the muffin tins and bake for 10 to 15 minutes (20 to 25 minutes for regular-size cupcakes) or until a toothpick inserted comes out clean. Set aside to cool in the pans on a wire rack and prepare the frosting.

7   Using an electric mixer on low speed, cream the butter, cream cheese, vanilla extract, and lemon juice. Gradually add the powdered sugar and continue blending until the frosting is smooth and light. Add the food coloring, if desired, and frost the cooled cupcakes. Decorate with sprinkles as desired.

Official Cooking Club Baby

Bundle of Joy

TEE TIME: SHARON
UNWRAPS A GIFT
FROM THE GANG

summer picnic

MENU

SWIMMING POOL SHRIMP
WITH CELERY ROOT

JUDY'S CHICKEN SALAD
WITH MANGO CHUTNEY

PAN BAGNAT

ORZO AND WILD RICE SALAD

ASIAN STRING BEAN SALAD

RASPBERRY LINZER SQUARES

A MOVEABLE FEAST

We take it outside

BEFORE SHARON GOT PREGNANT, she moved to New Jersey. And unlike our girly outbursts of joy when she told us that she and Ken were expecting, we were far from jubilant when we learned of the plan. Only Katherine (hands down the most gracious CC member) managed to eke out a congratulatory word. The rest of us, however, selfishly focused on what this out-of-state move would mean for the club.

That is, until Sharon told us there would be a pool. Now, for people who live in, say, Los Angeles or Tucson, an apartment complex with a pool may not seem like a reason to pop the bubbly. But in New York City, where a shower with good water pressure is never taken for granted, this was reason for celebration. Plus, Sharon added, the building had an enormous parklike backyard. Naturally, we started planning for the first annual Cooking Club picnic months in advance.

When the first Sunday in July finally arrived, Becky produced a picnic basket (yet another off-the-registry wedding gift that had been hibernating in her closet), complete with brightly colored containers for transporting the shrimp with mustard sauce, Asian string beans, and orzo salad that we decided had to be included in the menu. Also de rigueur: a French sandwich called a *pan bagnat,* which Cynthia had learned means "bathed bread." (That's French for "doesn't get soggy by lunch.") And because there was a unanimous decision to limit the use of mayonnaise in dishes that would be sitting in the sun, Lisa dug up a recipe for chicken salad made with mango chutney instead.

Since Sharon's new home was serviced by New York City public transit, we arrived in the suburbs by subway, bus, and sheer dint of Becky's navigational prowess. After wandering around the wooded areas behind the apartment complex for the perfect picnic spot, we settled on a mostly shady area with just the right amount of sunlight. And when we had polished off the crumbs of the Raspberry Linzer Squares (with help from Sharon's new neighbors, who had stopped to ogle the spread), we cleared space on the picnic blanket (really just an inexpensive linen tablecloth that Lucia picked up at a stoop sale) and began a round-robin backgammon tournament. (Incidentally, picnics are also a good time to fine-tune your Parcheesi or Boggle strategy.)

But board games in the shade only go so far on a hot summer day. It's probably not too hard to imagine what came next: CC members cannonballing off the diving board, chicken-racing across the shallow end, and Katherine doing water ballet. But even if you don't have a member with access to a pool, all you really need for a quality picnic is a nice shady spot of grass, tasty eats, and, of course, your best buddies.

summer picnic

PICNIC POINTERS

1. BRING A PRETTY TABLECLOTH: While we don't normally advocate trekking with table linens, they're worth the effort on a picnic. They make eating on the ground elegant, plus they help keep the ants away. (Be sure to bring a plastic drop cloth or a few garbage bags to layer underneath so members don't get soggy from sitting on ground that's damp or dewy.)

2. PACK A SHARP KNIFE: We learned that it can be much easier to bring foods whole (such as our tinfoil-wrapped *pan bagnat* or our linzer squares) and then cut them into single servings on site. But trying to slice a sub sandwich with a plastic spork just isn't going to cut it. (Literally.)

3. DON'T BE AFRAID OF WEIGHT GAIN: Some of the heavy extras—a bottle of wine, a bouquet of flowers, fancy sodas, and board games—can really make a picnic special. If the basket is hard to carry, invite a boyfriend or other Sherpa-type person to help carry the load.

SWIMMING POOL SHRIMP WITH CELERY ROOT

Unrefrigerated seafood initially seemed like a bad idea for a picnic, but we brought along a cooler and made sure the recipe included celery root, an addition that makes any food taste deliciously fresh. (Since no one got food poisoning, we've concluded that some picnic seafoods are safe.) Celery root is worth discovering, but the first time you try to find it, you may end up with jicama or even a round potato. What you're looking for is a round root vegetable with a thick, light brown peel. Slice or peel away the thick skin and then grate the celery root. If you can't track it down, you can substitute three finely chopped white inner stalks of celery. ▪ *Yield: 4 to 6 servings*

2 tablespoons fresh lemon juice
3 tablespoons extra-virgin olive oil
2 tablespoons mayonnaise
2 tablespoons whole-grain Dijon mustard
1 tablespoon smooth Dijon mustard
36 cooked medium shrimp (about 1½ pounds),
peeled and deveined
1 cup shredded arugula, sliced into ½-inch strips
1 cup peeled grated celery root
salt and freshly ground pepper to taste

1 To prepare the dressing, whisk together the lemon juice, olive oil, mayonnaise, and mustards in a small bowl.

2 In a large bowl, toss the shrimp, arugula, and celery root; add the dressing, tossing until mixed. Season with salt and pepper.

JUDY'S CHICKEN SALAD WITH MANGO CHUTNEY

At our friend Shari's baby shower, her mom, Judy Levin, cooked much of the food, and let's just say that everyone in attendance ate for two. This dish disappeared before even Judy's killer cheesecake black-bottom brownies were gone. For our picnic, we made the mango chutney here, but Judy uses Major Grey's mango chutney (available at the supermarket), and if you're in a rush, you should, too. ■ *Yield: 4 to 6 servings*

FOR THE CHUTNEY

3 mangoes, peeled and chopped
½ cup red wine vinegar
½ cup sugar
¼ cup golden raisins
1 tablespoon minced
peeled fresh ginger
½ teaspoon salt

FOR THE SALAD

4 boneless, skinless chicken breasts
(about 2 pounds), rinsed and patted dry
with paper towels

2 tablespoons mayonnaise
4 scallions (white parts plus 2 inches
of green), thinly sliced
1 carrot, shredded
½ cup sliced blanched almonds
1½ cups snow peas, rinsed and
cut into julienne strips
1 tablespoon minced fresh cilantro,
plus extra whole leaves
salt and freshly ground pepper to taste
lettuce leaves (such as Boston)
(optional)

1 To prepare the chutney, bring all the chutney ingredients to a boil in a large pot. Reduce the heat and simmer for 45 minutes, stirring the mixture frequently so it doesn't stick to the bottom of the pot. When done, remove from the heat and set aside. Let cool.

2 Bring a large pot of water to a boil. Add the chicken breasts and cook until the chicken is almost cooked through, about 7 to 9 minutes, depending on the thickness of the breasts. (You'll want to slightly undercook them, as they will continue to cook when you remove them from the water.)

3 Remove the chicken from the pot. When it's cool enough to handle, tear the chicken into pieces that are roughly 1-inch-wide (bite-size) chunks.

4 In a large bowl, mix ¾ cup cooled chutney (save the remainder for another use) with the mayonnaise and scallions. Add the chicken and toss to coat. Add the shredded carrot, almonds, snow peas, and minced cilantro, and toss again. Season with salt and pepper. Serve in a bowl lined with lettuce leaves and garnish with whole cilantro leaves.

summer picnic

PAN BAGNAT

The problem with picnic sandwiches: You make them in the morning, by noon they're mush, and you go straight for the cookies instead. But leave it to the French to solve both the texture issue and the all-too-common mayonnaise-in-the-sun fear factor. The name *pan bagnat* essentially means "bathed bread"; the sandwich is popular in places where people say "bathe" instead of "swim," like the Côte d'Azur. Made with a vinaigrette in lieu of mayonnaise, the sandwich is meant to sit around (in the shade or a cooler—don't push your luck) so that the flavors can meld.

■ *Yield: 4 to 6 servings*

1 sushi-grade tuna steak
(about 1 pound), rinsed and
patted dry with paper towels

salt and freshly ground pepper to taste

3 tablespoons extra-virgin olive oil

FOR THE VINAIGRETTE

2 tablespoons champagne vinegar

5 tablespoons extra-virgin olive oil

1 teaspoon herbes de Provence ❊

1 long, wide loaf crusty French bread
(avoid the super-skinny baguettes)

black olive tapenade
(about 2 to 3 tablespoons)

2 cups roughly chopped watercress

2 medium tomatoes, thinly sliced

2 hard-boiled eggs,
shelled and thinly sliced

salt and freshly ground pepper to taste

1 To prepare the tuna, season it with salt and pepper. Heat 3 tablespoons olive oil in a large skillet over medium-high heat. Cook the tuna in the skillet for 3 minutes on each side (the center should still be quite pink).

2 Remove the tuna from the pan and allow to cool for 15 minutes. When cooled, slice it into ¼-inch-wide pieces.

3 While the tuna is cooling, whisk together the vinaigrette ingredients in a small bowl.

4 Slice the bread lengthwise and scoop out some of the inside dough to create room for the fillings. Spread the inside of one side of the baguette with the tapenade and then drizzle both sides with the vinaigrette. Layer on the watercress, tuna, tomatoes, and eggs. Season with salt and pepper. Wrap the entire sandwich in aluminum foil, then slice into sections when ready to eat.

❊ If you can't find herbes de Provence, substitute ½ teaspoon dried oregano and ½ teaspoon dried tarragon.

ORZO AND WILD RICE SALAD

If cold rice makes you think of the sneeze-guard at your local supermarket salad bar, think again. This delicate orzo pasta with wild rice has been our go-to side dish in pressured cooking situations. (We're talking about any home-prepared meal that involves in-laws, the boss, or bachelor number 3.) Because it can be made ahead of time and served at room temperature, it makes getting dinner on the table infinitely easier. (In these situations, we like to serve it with a thin fillet of fish baked in an oven.) We brought it to our picnic because we just can't eat it often enough.

■ *Yield: 4 to 6 servings*

1 cup orzo pasta, uncooked
½ cup wild rice, uncooked
¼ teaspoon salt
1 cup fresh or frozen peas
⅓ cup chopped fresh parsley
1 tablespoon minced red onion

FOR THE DRESSING
⅓ cup extra-virgin olive oil
2 teaspoons fresh lemon juice
3 tablespoons white balsamic vinegar
salt and freshly ground pepper to taste

summer picnic

1   In separate pots, cook the orzo and wild rice according to the directions on the packages. When they are finished cooking, rinse with cold water and place both in a large bowl.

2   Add the salt to a small pot of water and bring to a boil. Add the fresh peas, cook for 1 to 2 minutes, then remove and rinse in a colander under cold water to stop the cooking. (If using frozen peas, prepare according to the directions on the package, then rinse under cold water.) Transfer the peas to a small bowl and add the parsley and onion. Set aside.

3   To prepare the dressing, whisk together the olive oil, lemon juice, and vinegar in a small bowl. Add about half the dressing to the orzo-rice mixture and stir until the mixture is coated with the dressing. Add the peas mixture and toss well. Dress to taste with the remainder of the dressing. Season with salt and pepper.

ASIAN STRING BEAN SALAD

We often joke that Lucia is our Liquid Pleasure Director, mixing up potent punches and divine drinks. Less well known outside of Cooking Club are her legendary salads, which have upstaged the main course on more than one occasion. These string beans are no exception—in fact, you might want to double the amount of the mouthwatering sesame-soy dressing and save it for use on a leafy salad at another meal. One note: Lucia used grape tomatoes, but cherry tomatoes (try using yellow, orange, and red ones for added color) can be substituted. ■ *Yield: 4 to 6 servings*

2 teaspoons salt
1½ pounds green beans, washed and ends trimmed
large bowl of ice water
1 tablespoon sesame seeds

FOR THE DRESSING
3 tablespoons rice vinegar
2 tablespoons soy sauce
1 teaspoon sugar
¼ cup canola oil
2 tablespoons sesame oil
salt and freshly ground pepper to taste

—

1 pint grape tomatoes, halved

1 Place 2 teaspoons salt in a large pot of water and bring to a boil. Add the beans.

2 Cook the beans until they are bright green and crisp-tender, about 4 minutes. When the beans are done, remove from the heat, strain in a colander, and immediately immerse in the ice water to stop the cooking.

3 Toast the sesame seeds by placing them in a skillet (no oil needed) over medium-high heat for 1 minute. Shake the pan a few times during cooking. Then remove from the heat and set aside to cool.

4 To prepare the dressing, whisk together the vinegar, soy sauce, and sugar in a small bowl. Whisk in the canola and sesame oils. Add the sesame seeds and season with salt and pepper to taste.

5 Place the beans and tomatoes in a large bowl, add about half the dressing, and toss until the vegetables are coated. Dress to taste with the remainder of the dressing.

RASPBERRY LINZER SQUARES

Linzer cookies and tortes are Austrian desserts marked by the addition of ground nuts (usually hazelnuts or almonds) to the flour. Our friend Beth's husband, Mark Zink, who just happens to be a pastry chef, told us that the secret to great Linzers is to grind the sugar with the nuts before baking to make both into finer particles. (For the same reason, it's important to use cake flour, which is finer than all-purpose flour.) We made bars because they're just so darn easy to bring to a picnic or potluck—you can prepare them in a disposable pan and then slice them into squares when you arrive. ■ *Yield: 2 dozen squares*

2 cups cake flour
¼ teaspoon baking powder
¼ teaspoon cinnamon
¾ cup sugar
½ cup sliced blanched almonds

14 tablespoons (1¾ sticks) unsalted butter, softened and cut into tablespoons
1 egg
¼ teaspoon vanilla
1 cup raspberry all-fruit jelly

1   Preheat the oven to 350 degrees.

2   In a medium bowl, sift together the flour, baking powder, and cinnamon.

3   Use a food processor to grind the sugar and the nuts together until the particles are very fine.

4   Add the butter to the sugar mixture in the processor and cream together. Add in the egg and vanilla. Process until combined.

5   Gradually add the flour mixture to the mixture in the processor, and process until just combined.

6   Remove one quarter of the dough and roll it out on a cutting board dusted with flour to a rectangle that is about 10 inches by 5 inches and ¼ inch thick. Place the cutting board with dough in the freezer for 15 minutes.

7   Spread the remaining dough into a 13-by-9-inch nonstick pan. Refrigerate the pan and dough for 10 minutes.

8   Remove the pan from the refrigerator and then cover the dough with jelly, spreading evenly.

9   Remove the cutting board from the freezer and slice the dough lengthwise into ½-inch wide slices. Lay these in a lattice pattern on top of the jelly.

10   Bake for 30 minutes, until the top and edges are golden. Allow to cool, then cut into individual square bars.

PIZZA IN A POT

'70s fondue party

MENU

DYNO MEATBALLS

FAR-OUT FRIED FONDUE

BLUE CHEESE DIP

COCKTAIL SAUCE

PIZZA IN A POT

CHOCOLATE FLUFFER FONDUE

PSYCHEDELIC POUND CAKE

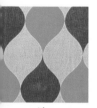

CHEESE BALL

Dipping into the past for a '70s fondue party

MAYBE IT'S COINCIDENCE, but the idea of a '70s-themed party came about only after Cynthia mentioned she bought two wrap dresses at the Diane von Furstenberg sample sale. Hmmm. Coincidence or not, once the idea was out there it didn't take long for e-mails to fly back and forth about all the groovy paraphernalia we could resurrect from our youth. Sharon said she'd bring her posters of Shaun Cassidy, Cynthia promised to pick up a six-pack of Fresca, and Lucia even offered to get the Dorothy Hamill wedge haircut (we all agreed that wasn't necessary). After Lisa said she'd let us borrow her collection of macramé headbands, we got down to business and discussed what we'd be dining on. Our research on "hot '70s dishes" revealed some rather unappetizing options: TV dinners, microwave specials, casseroles, quiches, and—get this—pasta primavera. Turns out that hip '70s people thought pasta with veggies was the greatest thing since sliced bread. Huh? As we tried to figure out where we could buy TV dinner trays, Katherine said, "Hey, jive turkeys, the decade's most decadent way to eat was clearly fondue!" We all thumped our heads in agreement, and '70s Fondue Fantasia was set.

Becky seemed the most versed in fondue since her family gathers around a pot of boiling oil every Christmas Eve to cook filet mignon to perfection. Derived from the French word *fondre,* which means "to melt," fondue is a pretty broad category. We had a heated debate over whether the keep-it-warm-over-an-open-flame version still counted or if you actually had to cook your meal in a pot to call it fondue. Katherine claimed both ways were acceptable and paraphrased one of the more popular books of the decade by saying "Hey, my fondue's OK, your fondue's OK."

To really get into the spirit, we broke out our bell-bottoms and Greg Brady door beads and sprawled (à la Carole King) on a shag carpet in Sharon's apartment. Becky even managed to borrow a giant orange beanbag from a friend, claiming no real '70s party would be complete without one. No real '70s party would be complete without some wacky t'backy either, but we figured a bowl of warm melted chocolate would have us giddy soon enough.

FUN WITH FONDUE

ONE POT DOES NOT FIT ALL FONDUES: The fondue pot you'll use for cheese or chocolate should be made of a heat-diffusing material such as ceramic or porcelain, either by itself or as an insert in a stainless steel pot. Such dainty fondues could scorch inside metal, and although we'll eat any kind of chocolate, the burnt version is our least favorite. Oil-based fondues should be done in an electric metal pot.

SAY YES TO WINE: When choosing a beverage to accompany your cheese fondue, skip the aqua. Allegedly, water will cause the cheese to congeal in your stomach, causing gastrointestinal problems later on. We also heard that any cold beverage could do the same. Even if you think it's a whole load of hoo-ha, why test this theory?

DON'T DROP YOUR DUNKER: There is a tradition that states if a woman loses her dipper in the pot, she has to kiss all the men at the table. We thought that was kind of sexist (and awkward to implement since the only men skulking around were husbands), so we just decided that whoever loses the most morsels scrubs the pot.

DO THE DIP RIGHT: Swirl a figure eight with your dipper when eating cheese or chocolate fondue—it'll be less likely to separate if it's constantly getting stirred. Also, occasionally scrape the bottom of the pot so the yummy goodness down there doesn't burn.

'70s fondue party

IN THE GROOVE:
LISA AND CYNTHIA
REVISIT THEIR
VINYL PAST. (YES,
THAT IS A KRISTY
McNICHOL 45.)

DYNO MEATBALLS

This delectable appetizer comes to the Cooking Club by way of the Meatball King of Chicago, Jeffrey Kaye. Keep these little guys warm in your fondue pot (a metal one is fine—just keep the heat low and stir it up every now and then) and put a bowl of toothpicks next to it. Why is it that food eaten with a toothpick doesn't seem as filling? For those who protest red meat, try subbing in 2 pounds of ground turkey. For our little Cooking Club, we cut this recipe, which is enough for a party of ten to twelve people, in half. ■ *Yield: 4 dozen meatballs*

FOR THE MEATBALLS	FOR THE SAUCE
¼ cup finely minced onion	3 tablespoons extra-virgin olive oil
1 tablespoon extra-virgin olive oil	3 cups beef stock
1 pound lean ground beef	5 tablespoons all-purpose flour
1 pound ground pork	½ cup beer
½ cup bread crumbs	2 teaspoons Worcestershire sauce
½ teaspoon nutmeg	
½ teaspoon allspice	
½ teaspoon freshly ground pepper	
1 tablespoon salt	
1 tablespoon Worcestershire sauce	
2 eggs	

1 Preheat the oven to 350 degrees.

2 In a medium pan, sauté the onion in 1 tablespoon olive oil until lightly browned.

3 In a large bowl, mix the onion, beef, pork, bread crumbs, nutmeg, allspice, pepper, salt, 1 tablespoon Worcestershire sauce, and eggs until blended.

4 Roll the beef mixture into 1-inch balls. Place on two ungreased cookie sheets and bake for 20 minutes, turning the meatballs over after fifteen minutes. (You can also sauté the meatballs in olive oil over medium-high heat in a large pan. Cook until well browned, about 4 minutes.)

5 To make the sauce, heat the olive oil in a medium saucepan over low heat. Whisk in the stock. Add the flour and continue to whisk until the sauce thickens. Stir in the beer and Worcestershire sauce.

6 When the meatballs are cooked, put them into a large (at least 3-quart) fondue pot and pour the sauce over them. Keep the fondue-pot heat on low.

'70s fondue party

FAR-OUT FRIED FONDUE

This started out as a classy tempura-style fondue but quickly degenerated into something, well, not so classy but way more fun. Since this is a '70s party, we thought it especially appropriate to up our saturated fat intake for the day because, let's face it, nobody cared about health back then. So we ditched the "No, it's not fried food, it's tempura" shtick as soon as Sharon's husband, Ken, started rummaging in the fridge for cheese to deep-fry. For a 3-quart metal fondue pot, use about 5 cups oil for frying, or enough so that the morsel is completely submerged (but not so much that it'll boil over if six CC members dunk their shrimp at the same time). ▪ *Yield: 6 servings*

FOR THE BATTER
2 cups all-purpose flour
1½ teaspoons garlic salt
1 teaspoon cayenne pepper
2 cups beer

—

vegetable oil for frying

SUGGESTED DIPPERS
1 pound cooked shrimp (25 to 30), peeled and deveined
1 small zucchini, sliced
1 small onion, cut into chunks
6 large mushroom caps, washed and cut in half
8 ounces fresh mozzarella cheese, cubed

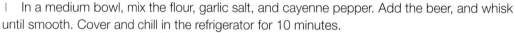

1 In a medium bowl, mix the flour, garlic salt, and cayenne pepper. Add the beer, and whisk until smooth. Cover and chill in the refrigerator for 10 minutes.

2 Fill an electric 3-quart fondue pot halfway with vegetable oil (the oil should be 2 inches deep). Heat until 350 degrees, or until a cube of bread browns in 30 seconds. You can also flick a drop of water into the pot to see if it sizzles.

3 Completely cover the dippers in the batter, then fry until browned.

BLUE CHEESE DIP

Dunk onions, zucchini, and mushrooms in this creamy dip. Have leftovers? Tear open a bag of potato chips and finish it off. ▪ *Yield: 1½ cups*

8 ounces cream cheese
1 cup milk
¼ teaspoon garlic powder
¼ teaspoon freshly ground pepper
½ teaspoon Worcestershire sauce
½ cup crumbled blue cheese

1 In a medium saucepan, melt the cream cheese with the milk over medium-low heat.
2 Add the garlic powder, pepper, and Worcestershire sauce; combine. Stir in the blue cheese. Let cool. Serve immediately or cover and refrigerate. The dip can be made a day ahead.
3 To serve the dip, separate it into a couple of small bowls or ramekins and spread them around the table.

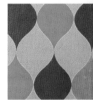

COCKTAIL SAUCE

This is a spicy traditional cocktail sauce that makes a great dip for fried shrimp and mozzarella cubes. To make sure it won't be too spicy, hide the Tabasco Sauce from Katherine.
▪ *Yield: 1¼ cups*

1 cup ketchup
2 tablespoons drained bottled horseradish
¼ teaspoon Tabasco Sauce
2 teaspoons fresh lemon juice
1 teaspoon Worcestershire sauce
salt and freshly ground pepper to taste

1 In a small bowl, whisk together all the ingredients. Serve immediately or cover and refrigerate. The sauce can be made a day ahead.
2 To serve the sauce, separate it into a couple of small bowls or ramekins and spread them around the table.

'70s fondue party

FLYING FORKS:
MAKE SURE
YOU SIT
CLOSEST TO
THE POT YOU
LIKE BEST

PIZZA IN A POT

The national dish of Switzerland is a delicious blend of Emmental and Gruyère cheeses, but the pungent scent is a bit akin to stinky feet. So as not to upset any noses, we decided to do something a little less offensive olfactory-wise. Someone suggested we go whole-hog '70s and mix a chunk of Velveeta with a packet of instant onion soup, but we opted to create a virtual pizza by adding tomatoes and herbs. Cheese fondue is notoriously finicky, and although it's easier to dump a bag of already shredded cheese in the pot, you'll get a much better melt if you buy a brick and shred it yourself. Warning to you dieters out there: Go full fat or go home. A low-fat cheese won't melt as well and will stick to the pot (not to mention it won't taste as good). To encourage a smoothly melted cheese, warm up the fondue pot by first adding hot water to it, then tossing the water out and drying the pot before pouring in the fondue. ■ *Yield: 4 to 6 servings*

1 cup shredded cheddar cheese
1 cup shredded Monterey Jack cheese
½ cup coarsely grated fresh
Parmigiano-Reggiano
1 teaspoon cornstarch, plus more,
if necessary
2 tablespoons unsalted butter
1 14½-ounce can diced tomatoes,
drained
2 cloves garlic, minced

1½ teaspoons crushed fennel seeds
1½ teaspoons chopped fresh oregano
3 tablespoons dry white wine
(like a Sauvignon Blanc or Chablis),
plus more, if necessary

SUGGESTED DIPPERS
pepperoni, sliced and halved
artichoke hearts, halved
garlic bread, cubed

1   In a large bowl, toss the cheddar, Monterey Jack, and Parmigiano-Reggiano cheeses and the cornstarch together. Set aside.

2   In a medium saucepan, melt the butter over low heat. Add the tomatoes, garlic, fennel seeds, and oregano. Bring to a simmer, stirring occasionally, until the liquid is evaporated, about 10 minutes. Remove from the heat.

3   In a large saucepan, heat the wine over low to medium heat until simmering, then add the cheese mixture by the handfuls, stirring continuously until completely melted. Don't let the cheese mixture boil.

4   Add the tomato mixture to the melted cheese mixture and transfer to a fondue pot. If the consistency is too thin, add up to a tablespoon of cornstarch that has been dissolved in a tablespoon of warm wine; stir. If the cheese becomes too thick, add some warmed wine and stir until smooth.

'70s fondue party

CHOCOLATE FLUFFER FONDUE

For her next birthday, Katherine asked if the Cooking Club would fill her tub with this delicious dessert so she could bathe in it. We considered it until we envisioned the cleanup. If you don't want to spring for a bottle of Frangelico (oooh, but it's worth it), you can substitute vanilla extract. If you're using a ceramic insert fondue pot, add a bit of water to the metal pot first to create a double boiler so that the chocolate doesn't burn. ■ *Yield: 4 to 6 servings*

12 ounces milk chocolate, chopped
½ cup heavy cream
3 tablespoons Frangelico liqueur
1 cup Marshmallow Fluff

l   Melt the chocolate and cream in a medium saucepan over medium heat. Whisk continuously until melted. Do not allow to burn. Stir in the Frangelico.

2   Transfer to a fondue pot and swirl in Marshmallow Fluff. Keep warm over low heat.

PSYCHEDELIC POUND CAKE

The tie-dyed ribbon of chocolate in this cake won't have you seeing things, but it will add some yummy flavor and keep your cake moist. And since Jell-O molds were all the rage in the '70s, swirling a box of Jell-O Instant Pudding into the batter seemed quite appropriate. We love chocolate fudge but are also fans of banana cream and French vanilla. ▪ *Yield: 20 to 24 servings*

16 tablespoons (2 sticks) unsalted butter, softened
2 cups sugar
2 cups all-purpose flour, sifted
2 tablespoons cornstarch
½ teaspoon cream of tartar
6 eggs
2 teaspoons vanilla extract
1 package chocolate fudge Jell-O Instant Pudding

1 Preheat the oven to 350 degrees. Adjust the oven rack to the middle level. Grease a tube pan with butter; set aside.

2 Using an electric mixer, cream the butter and sugar.

3 In a medium bowl, mix the flour, cornstarch, and cream of tartar. Add the eggs and flour mixture to the butter mixture in three batches (2 eggs with a third of the flour). Mix each batch for 1 minute, or until combined, then add the next batch. Mix in the vanilla extract. Pour two thirds of the batter into the tube pan.

4 Add the package of pudding to the remaining batter and mix well. Spoon the batter into the tube pan. With a knife, swirl throughout the batter.

5 Bake for about 60 minutes. Test the doneness with a toothpick. It should come out with moist crumbs clinging to it.

'70s fondue party

karaoke bachelorette party

MENU

BRITNEY'S SPEARS

WE GOT THE BEAN DIP

MISS AMERICAN PIE
BASIC DOUGH AND SAUCE

SPINACH AND GOAT CHEESE PIZZA

THAT'S THE WAY, UH-HUH, UH-HUH,
I LIKE MY PIZZA

JAMES BROWNIES

NOWHERE NEAR LIKE
A VIRGIN DAIQUIRI

GIRLS JUST WANT TO HAVE
FUN WITH SHOTS

HIT SINGLE

We make our bachelorette sing for her supper

EVEN THOUGH THE MAJORITY of CC are tone deaf (or at least sing like we are), that never seems to stop us from heading to the Karaoke Duet lounge in midtown Manhattan for many a raucous party (Becky's twenty-fifth and Cynthia's twenty-eighth birthdays were celebrated there). We always make up in enthusiasm what we lack for in pitch, but at the end of every session, when our throats are raw and our ears are ringing, our tummies are inevitably grumbling (off tune, no less). So when it came time to toast (and roast) Lucia's nuptials, we knew our planned night of singing (screaming? screeching?) the entire soundtrack of *Footloose* would require more than a bag of Fritos to sustain us.

We decided any food that accompanies wildly dancing and feathered-boa-waving women had to be easy to nosh on. Sad to say, some foods just don't hold up during a reenactment of *Flashdance*. Trying to eat bruschetta while doing the Running Man to "Maniac" will only result in tomato chunks in your wedding veil. So we said no-go to anything that required sharp knives (one round of "YMCA" would have us dropping to the floor for cover), fancy sauces, or anything that needed to be flambéed (although how great an addition to "Burning Down the House" would that make?). That meant Sharon's Baby's Got Baby Back Ribs recipe would have to wait until we did a Texas Rodeo theme and Lucia's Axl Rose–inspired Sweet Sausage O' Mine (while oddly appropriate for a bachelorette party) would have to wait until we did Favorite Foods of '80s Hair Bands. Instead, we opted for food that you didn't necessarily need utensils for, like pizza, dip, and skewers. And although Lisa was at the ready to bake an anatomically correct cake in keeping with bachelorette traditions, we thought bite-size brownies would be less offensive in case any mother-of-the-bride or sister-of-the-groom showed up.

Drinks, of course, are extremely important to loosening up vocal cords, as well as any Cooking Club member trying to remain dignified. Our Nowhere Near Like a Virgin Daiquiris are more than up for the job. And because you can't exactly sing Rod Stewart's "Da Ya Think I'm Sexy?" if you're wearing sweatpants and an apron, proper attire is paramount. Look for pleather, leather, vinyl, and sequined apparel. Finally, while the mission of a bachelorette party is to celebrate the last single days of a bride-to-be, it's also a good time to show off your cooking club prowess. You want to make sure the newly hitched member remembers exactly why she'll continue to leave her husband home alone on the first Sunday of every month—we did.

CC'S GREATEST HITS

lucia: I'm all about singing "White Wedding" by Billy Idol because July 27 *better* be a "nice day for a white wedding."
katherine: The only time I can wear my gold lamé cowboy hat in good conscience is while singing "Music" by Madonna.

lisa: "Spice Up Your Life" by the Spice Girls is on par with my cooking mantra: Always use an abundance of fresh herbs.
becky: "Electric Youth" by Debbie Gibson because I never get to say "zappin' it to ya" in casual conversation.

sharon: "Hungry Like the Wolf" by Duran Duran pretty much sums up my daughter Margot's eating habits.
cynthia: "Dancing Queen" by ABBA because, well, I am one. At least during karaoke parties.

karaoke bachelorette party

BRITNEY'S SPEARS

After tasting these little morsels in the middle of belting out, "Hit me, baby, one more time," a CC friend christened them after the Great Bare Belly. Brilliant, it turns out, since we couldn't think of anyone better to embody the spirit of a bachelorette party than Britney Spears. That said, it's really the Japanese who should be getting the credit here. Among the many debts we owe them (sushi, Playstation, Godzilla) is karaoke. To pay proper homage, we made Japanese yakitori, tasty chicken skewers that are served in snack bars all over Japan. To shake this appetizer up (although it's hard to shake it more than Britney), add scallions, leeks, or pearl onions to accompany the marinated chicken. Bonus: These spears make a darn good substitute for a microphone when someone (or Cynthia) is hogging the real one. ■ *Yield: 12 skewers*

12 wooden skewers

———

FOR THE MARINADE
1 cup soy sauce
1 cup saki
¼ cup sugar
2 tablespoons grated peeled fresh ginger
3 cloves garlic, minced
freshly ground pepper to taste

———

**4 boneless, skinless chicken breasts (about 1½ pounds),
rinsed and patted dry with paper towels, cut into 1-inch pieces**
2 8-ounce cans whole water chestnuts, drained
2 red bell peppers, seeded and cut into 1-inch pieces

I   Preheat the broiler. Adjust the oven rack to the top level. Soak the skewers in water for 1 hour.
2   In a small saucepan over medium heat, whisk together the soy sauce, saki, sugar, ginger, and garlic. Season with pepper. Bring to a boil and let simmer for 5 minutes. Remove from the heat and let cool.
3   Alternately spear the chicken, water chestnuts, and peppers onto the skewers. Place in a shallow dish. Pour the marinade over the skewered chunks, reserving the marinade runoff, and refrigerate for at least 30 minutes (can be left overnight).
4   Place the skewers on aluminum foil over a broiler pan and baste with the reserved marinade. Cook for 4 minutes, flipping once and basting again with the marinade.

WE GOT THE BEAN DIP

Any Go-Go's song always brings the house down, but pair it with this tasty dip and you might as well set the darn place on fire. It's so easy to make that if you run out midsong, you can whip up another batch in the same time it takes Katherine to sing "Bohemian Rhapsody." For dippers, use veggies such as baby carrots or toasted pita bread that's been brushed with olive oil. ■ *Yield: 4 to 6 servings*

2 14-ounce cans white cannellini beans, drained

3 cloves garlic

2 tablespoons extra-virgin olive oil

2 tablespoons fresh lemon juice

½ teaspoon cayenne pepper

½ teaspoon salt

1 tablespoon chopped fresh chives

In a food processor, combine the beans, garlic, olive oil, lemon juice, pepper, and salt, and chop until smooth. Pour into a small serving bowl and garnish with the chives.

karaoke bachelorette party

MISS AMERICAN PIE
BASIC DOUGH AND SAUCE

Bread baking is an art—one we didn't know. And although, yes, you could just buy some Pillsbury dough or a premade Boboli crust and call it a day, that's not really giving it the old college try now, is it? Besides, once you've made your own crust, you'll never go back to pizza dough in a tube.

FOR THE DOUGH

4 teaspoons extra-virgin olive oil

1 cup hot water (heated to 105 to 115 degrees)

1 tablespoon yeast

2 teaspoons salt

1½ teaspoons sugar

3 to 3½ cups all-purpose flour

2 teaspoons dried oregano

¼ cup grated fresh Romano cheese (optional)

■ *Yield: one 14-inch pie*

FOR THE TOMATO SAUCE

2 tablespoons extra-virgin olive oil

3 cloves garlic, chopped

1 28-ounce can crushed tomatoes in puree

½ teaspoon red pepper flakes

1 tablespoon chopped fresh basil, or 1½ teaspoons dried

salt and freshly ground pepper to taste

■ *Yield: 2 to 2½ cups*

(enough for two 14-inch pizzas)

1 To make the dough, coat an electric mixer bowl with 2 teaspoons of olive oil.

2 Add the hot water (which must be between 105 and 115 degrees) to the mixing bowl.

3 Add the yeast and whisk until dissolved. Add the salt and sugar; whisk to blend.

4 Add 2 cups flour. Attach a dough hook to the mixer and mix the dough on low speed. Add more flour as needed to create a ball of dough that is neither sticky nor dry. Add the oregano and Romano cheese, if desired, to the dough. Mix on low to combine.

5 Remove the dough and, using your hands, gather it into a ball.

6 Pour 2 teaspoons of olive oil in the mixing bowl and swish the dough around so it's well oiled. Cover the bowl with a towel and let sit for 1 hour, until the dough is doubled in size.

7 To make the sauce, heat 2 tablespoons olive oil in a large saucepan over medium heat and sauté the garlic until lightly browned.

8 Stir in the tomatoes, red pepper flakes, and basil, and bring to a simmer. Season with salt and pepper. Simmer, uncovered, stirring occasionally, for 20 minutes, until the sauce is reduced to about 2½ cups. The sauce will keep, covered and chilled, for up to 5 days.

9 When the dough has risen, punch it down and leave, covered, for another 10 minutes. On a lightly floured surface, roll out the dough into the shape of your pizza pan. Ladle 1 to 1¼ cups sauce on the dough. (See our two pizza recipes on pages 112 and 114).

BECKY TOSSES PIZZA DOUGH
BEFORE GETTING "SAUCY" AT
OUR BACHELORETTE PARTY

SPINACH AND GOAT CHEESE PIZZA

To add even more flava to this pizza, dab a great olive oil on the crust right before you pop it in the oven. No pastry brush in your kitchen? We didn't have one either, but a clean synthetic-bristle makeup brush subbed in beautifully. For variety, try different flavors of goat cheese. We liked the garlic and herbs best. ■ *Yield: one 14-inch pizza*

FOR THE TOPPING
1½ tablespoons extra-virgin olive oil

2 cloves garlic, chopped

4 cups (packed) spinach leaves, rinsed well and
patted dry with paper towels

2 teaspoons chopped fresh rosemary

1 3-ounce package soft goat cheese

—

1 Miss American Pie Basic Dough and Sauce (page 110)

cornmeal for the baking stone

I Preheat the oven to 450 degrees. Adjust the oven rack to the bottom level.

2 Heat the olive oil in a large pan over medium heat and sauté the garlic. Add the spinach and stir until wilted, about 2 minutes. Stir in the rosemary. Remove from the heat.

3 Evenly sprinkle the spinach mixture and goat cheese on the prepared pie. Brush the edges of the dough with olive oil, if desired.

4 Let rise for 20 minutes. Sprinkle cornmeal on a pizza stone, place the pizza on top, and bake for 14 minutes, until the crust has browned.

LUCIA (BOTTOM RIGHT), THE BRIDE-TO-BE, AND THREE ASPIRING PAT BENATARS

THAT'S THE WAY, UH-HUH, UH-HUH, I LIKE MY PIZZA

This is a perfect base pizza on which to pile your favorite toppings. If your cooking club is somewhat pizza incompatible, as ours is (Lisa: "No meat, no peppers"; Sharon: "Me no like olives"; Katherine: "What do you mean it's weird to have oysters on pizza?"), set out different toppings and let your finicky friends decorate their side of the pie. ■ *Yield: one 14-inch pizza*

FOR THE TOPPING
chopped fresh oregano leaves, to taste
1 cup shredded mozzarella cheese
½ cup shredded sharp cheddar cheese
¼ cup grated fresh Romano cheese

———

1 Miss American Pie Basic Dough and Sauce (page 110)
additional toppings (optional)
cornmeal for the baking stone

1 Preheat the oven to 450 degrees. Adjust the oven rack to the bottom level.
2 In a large bowl, toss the oregano, mozzarella, cheddar, and Romano cheeses together.
3 Sprinkle the cheese mixture on the prepared pie; add additional toppings, if desired.
4 Let rise for 20 minutes. Sprinkle cornmeal on a pizza stone, place the pizza on top, and bake for 14 minutes, until the crust has browned and the cheese has melted.

JAMES BROWNIES

The original name of this ooey-gooey dessert was Brick House Brownies, but that was only because we overcooked the first batch by about an hour, thanks to a riveting episode of *The Bachelor*. Then Bad-to-the-Bone Brownies were born due to an oven that was off by about 100 degrees. Finally, Becky's friend and baked-goods-extraordinaire Jenny Kaye stepped in and said, "Papa's got a brand new bag o' brownies," and whipped up this batch with chunks of English toffee. One bachelorette party and Lisa singing "Sex Machine" at the top of her lungs later, James Brownies were born. After one bite of these, we guarantee you'll feel good. ■ *Yield: 16 brownies*

FOR THE BATTER
8 tablespoons salted butter
¾ cup semisweet chocolate chips
4 large eggs
2 teaspoons vanilla extract
1¼ cups sugar
1 cup all-purpose flour
1 cup chopped English toffee pieces
(a little less than 4 1.4-ounce Skor bars)

FOR THE FROSTING
4 tablespoons (½ stick) unsalted butter
¾ cup semisweet chocolate chips

1   Preheat the oven to 350 degrees. Adjust the oven rack to the middle level. Grease a 9-by-9-inch pan.

2   Melt the butter and ¾ cup chocolate chips in a small saucepan, stirring frequently. Remove from the heat and allow to cool.

3   In a large bowl, beat the eggs, vanilla extract, and sugar. Add the cooled chocolate mixture; combine. Stir in the flour until smooth. Add ½ cup toffee to the batter. Pour into the prepared pan.

4   Bake for 28 to 30 minutes. Test the doneness with a toothpick. When it comes out with moist crumbs clinging to it, remove the brownies and let cool for 1 hour.

5   To make the frosting, melt 4 tablespoons butter and ¾ cup chocolate chips in a small saucepan. Allow to cool.

6   Spread the frosting over the cooled brownies. Sprinkle the remaining toffee on top.

karaoke bachelorette party

NOWHERE NEAR LIKE A VIRGIN DAIQUIRI

Two glasses of this and you just might be able to hit a Mariah Carey high note. The secret to the great taste is the homemade sour mix. ▪ *Yield: 2 drinks*

FOR THE SOUR MIX
1 12-ounce can frozen-concentrate limeade
1 12-ounce can frozen-concentrate lemonade
12 ounces water (just fill up one of the cans)

———

4 ounces lemon-flavored rum (like Bacardi Limón)
2 cups frozen raspberries
1 cup ice cubes
whipped cream (optional)

1   To make the sour mix, stir the limeade, lemonade, and water together in a pitcher.

2   In a blender, combine the rum, raspberries, 6 ounces (about ¾ cup) sour mix, and ice. Blend until smooth.

3   Add a dollop of whipped cream to each drink for garnish, if desired.

GIRLS JUST WANT TO HAVE FUN WITH SHOTS

If your bride isn't into the prerequisite tequila body shot, this one will have her singing "Copacabana" in no time. ▪ *Yield: 6 shots*

1 cup crushed ice
6 ounces vodka
3 ounces Chambord
3 ounces sour mix

I   In a shaker, add the ice and pour in the vodka, Chambord, and sour mix.

2   Shake vigorously, then pour into six shot glasses through a sieve. Discard the ice.

karaoke bachelorette party

halloween

MENU

BE-DEVILED EGGS

HAUNTED HOT MULLED CIDER

BAT WING PASTA SALAD
WITH EYE OF NEWT

THAI SAUSAGE GOBLINS

SPIDER COOKIES

THE GREAT PUMPKIN
POPCORN BALLS

MONSTER BASH

Scaring up treats for the spookiest of celebrations

WHAT'S MORE FUN than Halloween? Nothing! We can't think of anything better than dressing up in weird outfits and having carte blanche in the candy department for the month of October. Maybe it's the cool, crisp chill in the autumn air, maybe it's something as simple as the sugar high, but we're batty for this ridiculous holiday.

Lucia, our resident Halloween freak, can recite every costume she's worn since eighth grade (the previous years being a simple little-girl rotation of Princess and Ballerina). She even has the history down—a fact we find about as frightening as the Headless Horseman's midnight ride (the old cartoon version of which used to scare the daylights out of us, to be honest). The bottom line is, people used to believe that on October 31 ghosts came back to earth to wreak a little havoc: They caused your garden-variety mischief, damaged crops, and looked for bodies to inhabit. Now, if you were under the impression that spirits were about to *inhabit your body,* wouldn't you dress up in a spooky costume and parade around town boisterously to frighten away these would-be body snatchers? So would we.

Spirits notwithstanding, our Halloween experiences have eerily similar parallels. All of us have had our share of indelible costume trauma. Cynthia is still smarting from that day long ago when her only wish was to be Princess Leia, but arriving too late at the costume shop, she wound up instead as a dejected, cross-dressing Luke. There have been successes, too, however. Thanks to some formidable hair product, Lisa's *There's Something about Mary* portrayal had fellow revelers shouting "Mary!" all the way across Broadway. And

Katherine's major masquerade coup? A prettier Pocahontas we have never seen. As far as parading around town goes, we've got that covered, too. We hear that Becky went "trick-or-treating" well into her teenage years and was known to impose candy tariffs on all the little unsuspecting ghosts and goblins of Arlington Heights, Illinois.

But, of course, no one wants to be all dressed up with nothing to eat. At our Halloween parties, we like to create a casual menu rather than a full sit-down dinner. We learned this one year when Sharon showed up as a Rubik's Cube—which is not an easy outfit to maneuver in, let alone manage to fit between you and the dining room table. We have found that hors d'oeuvres and salads aren't too tricky to handle if you're wearing, say, a gorilla suit. We also like to scatter baskets of candy around our apartments to go along with our own spooky desserts, like popcorn balls and spider cookies. All of which can easily be eaten while standing and chatting with whatever ghoulish guests glide your way. And when inviting folks to your spine-tingling soiree, always remember our three-word edict: "Costumes strenuously encouraged." It will ensure that everyone has a monstrously good time.

HALLOWEEN HOW-TO'S

1. Trust us on this: Your party will be ten times more fun if people dress up. Yes, it can be silly, and not everyone will comply (or get any candy, if you want to play hardball), but you'll be surprised at how creative your friends can be.

2. Make sure to serve food that won't rot teeth on contact along with all the sweet stuff, especially if you're also serving spooky cocktails.

3. Carving pumpkins and bobbing for apples can be fun in large groups. If you're five. Large knives in unsupervised situations are a questionable idea, and who ever liked sticking their face in a bucket of cold water the first time around?

4. Have a costume contest instead! If someone actually made it to your house dressed as a Teenage Mutant Ninja Turtle, don't they deserve a little recognition? Of course they do. Choose a reliable set of judges and a list of categories, and go wild.

BE-DEVILED EGGS

These much maligned hors d'oeuvres often get a bad rap. We say "boo!" to food snobs, however, and serve them all the time. Beware of these particular little demons—they're sky-high on the heat index. ▪ *Yield: 24 deviled eggs*

12 hard-boiled eggs
½ cup mayonnaise (low fat OK)
3 teaspoons spicy brown mustard

2 tablespoons Tabasco Sauce
¼ cup chopped fresh chives, for garnish

1   Cut the eggs in half lengthwise. Remove the yolks from the whites, and place the yolks in a medium bowl. Reserve the egg white "shells."
2   Add the mayonnaise, mustard, and Tabasco Sauce, and mix well with a fork.
3   Place a dollop of the yolk mixture in each egg white "shell."
4   Sprinkle with the chives and serve immediately.

HAUNTED HOT MULLED CIDER

The smell of this hot mulled cider when simmering on the stove never fails to catapult Cynthia into that collegiate fantasy in which she's all wrapped up in a wool sweater and scarf, walking across a bucolic American campus, carrying her travel mug of cider to class. Since fall is always all too fleeting, relish it by brewing up a cauldron of this autumnal elixir. It may just cast the same spell upon you. ▪ *Yield: 8 to10 servings*

8 cups apple cider
1 teaspoon allspice
1 cinnamon stick
¼ cup firmly packed dark brown sugar

16 whole cloves
1 orange, cut into eighths
1 cup dark rum

1   Pour the apple cider into a large stockpot and simmer for about 10 minutes on medium heat. Add the allspice, cinnamon stick, and dark brown sugar, and stir until blended.
2   Stick 2 whole cloves into the rind of each orange slice. Add to the stockpot and stir.
3   Stir in the rum. Let brew for another 5 to 10 minutes. Ladle into mugs and serve hot.

BAT WING PASTA SALAD WITH EYE OF NEWT

This simple pasta salad can be prepared in the blink of a black cat's eye. If you have trouble finding bat wings or the eye of newt, try substituting bow-tie pasta and green olives stuffed with pimientos, respectively. Neither is as delicious or as protein-rich as the former, but, visually, both could fool anyone not in-the-know. ■ *Yield: 8 to 10 servings*

FOR THE PASTA SALAD
1 pound bow-tie pasta

2 tablespoons extra-virgin olive oil

1 8-ounce package feta cheese, diced (about 1½ cups)

2 orange bell peppers, seeded and diced (about 2 cups)

1 19-ounce can black beans, drained and rinsed

1 6-ounce can manzanilla olives stuffed with pimientos

FOR THE DRESSING
1 tablespoon smooth Dijon mustard

1 teaspoon firmly packed light brown sugar

¼ cup red wine vinegar

½ cup extra-virgin olive oil

1 teaspoon dried basil

1 teaspoon dried thyme

salt and freshly ground pepper to taste

halloween

1 Cook the pasta according to the instructions on the package. Sprinkle with 2 tablespoons olive oil, toss, set aside, and allow to cool for about 10 minutes.

2 Combine the pasta, cheese, bell peppers, beans, and olives in a large bowl.

3 For the dressing, whisk together the mustard, sugar, and vinegar in a small bowl. Slowly whisk in ½ cup olive oil until well mixed. Add the herbs and season with salt and pepper.

4 When ready to serve, drizzle the dressing over the pasta and toss.

THAI SAUSAGE GOBLINS

This is an excellent recipe for a light, fresh sausage that when cooked alone is delicious on the grill during the summer. We went a step further, though, and mummified the patties by wrapping them in a blanket of dough and adding two beady peppercorn eyes. One look at our little goblins as they emerged from the oven lined up like mini soldiers and—much like Dr. Frankenstein must have felt upon witnessing his awesome creation—we reeled at the intoxicating power of giving life to . . . a sausage patty. ■ *Yield: 28 hors d'oeuvres*

1 pound ground pork
2 teaspoons minced shallots
⅓ cup chopped fresh cilantro
1 teaspoon minced garlic
1 tablespoon grated peeled fresh ginger
1½ tablespoons fresh lime juice
¼ cup sesame seeds
1 tablespoon crushed red pepper
1 teaspoon freshly ground pepper
1 teaspoon salt
2 to 3 tablespoons vegetable oil
1 8-ounce package Pillsbury crescent rolls
whole peppercorns, for decoration

1 Preheat the oven to 375 degrees.

2 Using your hands, combine all the ingredients except the oil, rolls, and peppercorns in a large bowl. Form into balls about the size of a golf ball, then flatten each into an oblong patty shape.

3 Heat the oil in a large, heavy skillet. Fry the patties over medium-high heat for about 4 minutes per side, until cooked through. (Or, cook over the grill for a delicious charcoal taste.)

4 Allow the patties to cool, about 10 minutes. When cool, cut in half horizontally. Wrap each half-patty with half the amount of dough of 1 roll.

5 Stand the patties up on an ungreased cookie sheet and add 2 peppercorns for eyes.

6 Bake according to the crescent roll package instructions, about 10 minutes or until browned.

SPIDER COOKIES

Lucia used to make a version of these cookies with her friend Sandy Siegel during the days when trading stickers was the ultimate hobby. The best part about them is that the recipe is oven-free, so if you live in a tiny apartment like most of us do, it won't heat up to Gates-of-Hell-like temperatures. The other great thing is, like more than half of the recipes in this chapter, these critters actually stare back at their maker. We adore the Sno-Caps eyes and the spidery licorice legs, but even without them this cookie can still stand on its own. ■ *Yield: 3 dozen cookies*

1½ cups sugar
⅓ cup unsweetened baking cocoa
4 tablespoons (½ stick) unsalted butter
½ cup milk
1 teaspoon vanilla extract
3 cups plain, instant oatmeal, uncooked
black licorice strings, cut into 1½-inch pieces, for decoration
72 Sno-Caps candies, for decoration

1   In a medium saucepan, bring the sugar, cocoa, butter, and milk to a boil for 1 minute, stirring occasionally.

2   Remove from the heat. Allow the mixture to cool for 5 minutes.

3   Add the vanilla extract and stir in the oatmeal a little at a time.

4   Roll the dough into balls slightly larger than a golf ball. Place on cookie sheets lined with waxed paper until all the dough has been used.

5   As the cookies are cooling, poke the licorice strings into the cookie sides, 3 per side. Affix 2 Sno-Caps to one end of each cookie for a pair of eyes.

6   After each sheet of cookies has been decorated, allow to cool in the refrigerator for at least 2 hours before serving.

LICORICE WHIPS
GIVE THESE SPIDER
COOKIES LEGS

THE GREAT PUMPKIN POPCORN BALLS

We're split fifty-fifty on the topic of whether popcorn balls are traditional Halloween fare. Katherine tried to convince us that some store-bought concoction called Poppycock is the supreme popcorn delicacy, but after trying these marshmallow wonders, she understood that that belief was, well, poppycock. If Linus had had one of these with him in the pumpkin patch instead of that damn blanket, we're sure the Great Pumpkin would've shown up. ■ *Yield: 4 popcorn balls*

3 tablespoons unpopped popcorn kernels
1 to 2 tablespoons vegetable oil
3 tablespoons unsalted butter
1 10½-ounce package minimarshmallows
½ teaspoon salt
7 drops yellow food coloring
2 drops red food coloring
mini M&M's candies, for decoration
green gumdrops, for decoration

1   In a heavy medium saucepan, pour in the oil and heat the kernels over high heat. The oil should just cover the bottom of the pan and be no more than 1 kernel deep. Cover with a lid. As soon as you hear the first pops, begin shaking the pan back and forth over the burner; shake constantly.

2   When you can count 3 to 4 seconds between pops, remove from the heat.

3   Pour the popcorn into a large bowl. Allow to cool and set aside.

4   In a large saucepan, melt the butter and marshmallows, stirring occasionally, until smooth and creamy. Add the salt.

5   Stir in both food colorings. Experiment with amounts of each to create the perfect shade of pumpkin orange. The number of drops may vary.

6   Gradually add the popcorn, stirring in a little at a time. Remove from the heat. Allow to cool for 5 minutes.

7   With greased hands, carefully form the popcorn mixture into balls the size of a baseball. Place on waxed paper–lined cookie sheets. Refrigerate for 5 to 10 minutes to cool and set.

8   Once set, decorate with the M&M's candies for faces and the gumdrops for pumpkin stems. Return to the refrigerator and allow to harden for about 1 hour.

THIS HALLOWEEN
PEAPOD (A.K.A.
MARGOT FREDMAN)
IS CUTE ENOUGH
TO EAT!

holiday dinner

MENU

TRADITIONAL TURKEY

CHALLAH STUFFING WITH
CRANBERRIES

CARROT SOUFFLÉ

POTATO LATKES

ICED ALMOND BARS

MILK PUNCH

SEASON'S EATINGS

We gather together for holiday cheer

OVER THE YEARS, the Cooking Club annual holiday party has taken many different forms—there was the time we did the twelve cocktails of Christmas and appetizers (we drew a big crowd for that one), the karaoke caroling party (which nearly got Becky and Steve evicted from their apartment), and even an intimate gathering of seven (the year Steve was our only guest). Most recently, in a fit of nostalgia, we threw a truly traditional holiday supper, minus any hair-pulling little cousins or prying Great Aunt Ednas. In honor of the occasion, Sharon finally opened her wedding china (which had been sitting in boxes since she and Ken were married five years ago) and we celebrated in style.

We all agreed that the debut of the wedding china warranted some special fare, so a roast turkey was the first item on the menu. This wasn't the first time Cooking Club had tackled turkey. One November we had the questionable idea of having a pre-Thanksgiving feast the Sunday before the holiday. Sharon unwittingly bought a thirteen-pound turkey for the six of us, so we ate for two and took home leftovers. Four days later, we did it again with our families and quickly learned why Thanksgiving only comes once a year.

Although our holiday turkey definitely took center stage, the side dishes were hardly ignored. Lisa knew her challah stuffing was a hit when Katherine, who was initially crushed at the thought of stuffing without oysters, went back for seconds. Sharon stunned us all when she broke out the frying pan (she's known for her fat-free fare, so we had never seen her fry anything) to make the potato latkes that she grew up eating every Hanukkah. (She later confessed to having used two rolls of paper towels to soak up the excess oil.) And Katherine's Carrot Soufflé, which is more dessert than vegetable, was an instant winner. Lucia showed up with a homemade milk punch, a fantastic concoction that showed how far we had come since our first holiday party, at which we served store-bought eggnog.

But no holiday meal would be complete without a delectable dessert, and Becky's in-laws' special almond tart did not disappoint. Steve's great-grandmother got this recipe in Sweden in 1956, where she bought the tins needed to make the tarts. Since Becky had no time for a repeat trip (although she did look into the price of plane tickets), she adapted this recipe and made Iced Almond Bars. We even managed to save one for Steve, who confirmed that they were just as delicious as he remembered.

TURKEY TALK

WHAT SIZE TURKEY SHOULD I BUY? Purchase 1 pound per person (a 12-pound bird should serve twelve people). Although if you want leftovers (and who doesn't?), estimate about 1½ pounds per person.

HOW SHOULD THE TURKEY BE THAWED? Fresh turkeys are available for the chef who can't wait for a frozen turkey to thaw. Just be aware that they come with an expensive price tag. Frozen turkeys should be thawed in the refrigerator (*not* at room temperature, to avoid the growth of bacteria) in their original sealed wrapping and need approximately 24 hours per 5 pounds of turkey. (A frozen 15-pound turkey needs 3 days to thaw.) Cooks strapped for time can submerge the sealed turkey in cold water and change the water every 30 minutes. The turkey will then take 30 minutes per pound to thaw.

(A 15-pound turkey would only need 7½ hours.)

WHEN IS THE TURKEY DONE? According to the National Turkey Federation (yes, there actually is a federation), you should roast a turkey in a 325-degree oven until a meat thermometer indicates 180 degrees in the thigh and 170 degrees in the breast. But the best place to find the exact cooking time is simply on the back of the turkey packaging.

holiday dinner

TRADITIONAL TURKEY

After Cynthia made her first turkey, she realized what experienced Thanksgiving makers already knew: Preparing it is surprisingly easy. There is no sauce to prepare, no extra ingredients to buy, and very little prep to be had. In fact, as long as you can get past the emotional anguish of removing the giblets and neck from the turkey, the hardest part is visiting your bird every thirty minutes to baste it with its juices—although for us it was finding an oven big enough to hold a 12-pound turkey. ■ *Yield: 8 (with leftovers) to 12 servings*

1 12-pound turkey, thawed
2 tablespoons unsalted butter, at room temperature
dash of garlic powder
dash of paprika
salt and freshly ground pepper to taste
2 large onions, cut into large chunks
1 teaspoon cornstarch (optional) for gravy

1   Preheat the oven to 325 degrees.
2   Remove the giblets and neck, rinse the turkey, then pat it dry with paper towels. Place it, breast side up, in a large roasting pan.
3   Spread the butter all over the outside of the turkey. Sprinkle the garlic powder and paprika on top; season with salt and pepper. Add the onions to the sides of the pan and inside the turkey cavity.
4   Cook the turkey, uncovered, for 3½ hours or until a meat thermometer registers 180 degrees in the thigh. Baste every 30 minutes with the pan drippings.
5   If desired, make a simple gravy by combining the pan drippings, cooked onions, and cornstarch.

CHALLAH STUFFING WITH CRANBERRIES

Challah is a traditional egg-rich bread served for the Jewish Sabbath. Because this bread starts out sweetened by either sugar or honey, it is a nice base for stuffing (or French toast, but that's another recipe). And because the consistency of this bread is so thick and doughy, it soaks up the vegetables and chicken broth, making it moist. Lisa used dried cranberries for color and a hint of sweetness, but dried cherries or raisins work just as well. And the best part of this dish is it will form a nice foundation with which to soak up all the holiday libations, such as Milk Punch (page 141). ■ *Yield: 4 to 6 servings*

1½ teaspoons vegetable oil
2 to 3 stalks celery, sliced
1 large onion, chopped
2 cloves garlic, minced
3 carrots, shredded
1 pound mushrooms, destemmed
6 slices challah bread
2 eggs, beaten
1 cup chicken broth
6 ounces sweetened dried cranberries (or Cranraisins)
salt and freshly ground pepper to taste

1   Preheat the oven to 350 degrees. Grease a 13-by-9-inch pan. (A smaller, deeper pan can also be used.)

2   In a large skillet, heat the oil and fry the celery, onion, garlic, and carrots. Add the mushrooms after the other vegetables have softened.

3   Tear each challah slice into pieces and place in a large bowl. Add the eggs and fried vegetable mixture.

4   Pour in the chicken broth until the stuffing is moist. (You may not need the full cup.) Sprinkle in the cranberries; season with salt and pepper.

5   Spoon into the prepared pan and cook for 30 minutes.

holiday dinner

CARROT SOUFFLÉ

Even though carrots are a vegetable, there is technically nothing healthy about this soufflé. But we found that with all the eggs, butter, sugar, and cinnamon used, we were hard-pressed to find a better-tasting dish to go with our feast. So you could cook up some steamed veggies on the side, but don't pass up this beautiful and delicious recipe. Hey, it's the holidays after all. You're going to be bundled up until spring! ■ *Yield: 4 to 6 servings*

1½ pounds frozen crinkle-cut carrots
3 eggs
5 tablespoons all-purpose flour
1 teaspoon baking powder
8 tablespoons (1 stick) unsalted butter, chopped
¼ cup sugar
½ teaspoon cinnamon

1   Preheat the oven to 350 degrees. Grease an 8-inch round casserole dish.
2   In a large stockpot, boil the carrots in water for 10 to 15 minutes; drain and mash into small chunks (yielding about 3 to 3½ cups mashed carrots).
3   Add the eggs, flour, baking powder, butter, and sugar to the mashed carrots. Mix until the butter is softened.
4   Pour the mixture into the prepared dish, and bake for 45 minutes, until the soufflé hardens into a cakelike texture.
5   Cool slightly, then sprinkle the cinnamon on top.

POTATO LATKES

Potato latkes (or pancakes) are traditionally made during Hanukkah, the Jewish Festival of Lights. It's the custom to serve foods that have been fried in oil as a remembrance of the miracle that took place more than two thousand years ago, when a handful of Jews were victorious over their enemies and when a little jar of oil that was really sufficient for only one day burned miraculously for eight. Although frying is not Sharon's forte, she jumped at the chance to make these for Cooking Club as her own personal remembrance of Hanukkah dinners from growing up. Now she makes them smaller as hors d'oeuvres and watches them miraculously disappear. ■ *Yield: 6 to 8 servings*

6 large potatoes (unpeeled baking potatoes
work best), washed well

1 to 1½ large onions

3 eggs

¾ cup all-purpose flour

2 to 3 teaspoons salt

freshly ground pepper to taste

1 cup vegetable oil for frying

———

applesauce and/or sour cream for serving

1 Grate the potatoes and onions in a food processor or blender.

2 Transfer the potato mixture to a large bowl and add the eggs and flour; season with the salt and pepper.

3 Heat ¼ cup oil in a large skillet until the oil is hot but not smoking. Drop approximately 2 tablespoons of the potato mixture into the oil.

4 Fry the pancakes for 3 to 4 minutes per side, removing them from the oil when they have become golden in color and achieve a crispy texture. Place between paper towels and gently press to remove the excess oil. Repeat the process until the potato mixture is finished, adding more oil when necessary.

5 Delicious served with applesauce and/or sour cream.

ICED ALMOND BARS

After we oooohed and aaahed about how delicious we thought this dessert was, Becky filled us in on a little cookie bar secret. They are even better frozen! Lucky for us she had a stash for each of us to try. The rest of the night was spent coming up with other foods we like to eat frozen. The hands-down winner: Milky Ways. ▪ *Yield: about 12 bars*

FOR THE COOKIE

2 cups sugar

3 sticks unsalted butter, softened

3 eggs

2½ cups all-purpose flour

½ teaspoon salt

1½ teaspoons almond extract

6 ounces slivered almonds, without skins, ground in a food processor

FOR THE GLAZE

2 cups powdered sugar

2 tablespoons unsalted butter, softened

½ teaspoon almond extract

3 tablespoons milk

maraschino cherries (optional)

1 Preheat the oven to 375 degrees. Grease a 13-by-9-inch baking dish.

2 Using an electric mixer, cream together 1 cup sugar, 2 sticks butter, and 1 egg in a large mixing bowl. Add the flour, salt, and 1 teaspoon almond extract. Mix the dough with your hands to combine thoroughly.

3 Pat the mixture firmly into the prepared dish. Set aside.

4 Using an electric mixer, cream together 1 stick butter, 1 cup sugar, 2 eggs, and ½ teaspoon almond extract (you can use the same large bowl to help with clean-up). Add the ground almonds and stir.

5 Pour this mixture onto the cookie crust and spread until evenly distributed. Bake for 20 minutes.

6 To make the glaze, mix the powdered sugar, butter, almond extract, and milk in a medium bowl.

7 Once the cookies are cool, pour the glaze on top. Cut into bars. Garnish each cookie with a cherry on top, if desired. (Another option: After the cookies cool, cut them into bars first and then glaze each cookie individually to allow the glaze to drip over the side.)

holiday dinner

MILK PUNCH

At Cornell, alma mater of our Liquid Pleasure Director's parents, Milk Punch was originally served during a four-day party weekend called Junior Week. Formal dinners, concerts, and parades were the order of the day. And Milk Punch was the drink of the hour. Or, to be accurate, the drink of the wee hours. It was typically served late at night or—get this—for breakfast. We found it is a great alternative to eggnog any time of day. ▪ *Yield: 8 drinks*

1 quart whole milk
4 ounces rum
4 ounces brandy
1 teaspoon sugar
4 hefty scoops of ice cream
nutmeg to taste

I Pour the milk into a pitcher. Add the rum, brandy, and sugar and stir. Check portions and alter according to taste.

2 Add the ice cream (vanilla is de rigueur; chocolate is acceptable; anything else is suspect) and sprinkle with nutmeg.

holiday dinner

POACHED EGGS WITH
SPINACH AND ARTICHOKE
HEARTS, HOME FRIES,
CITRUS MINT FRUIT SALAD,
AND BLOODY MARY

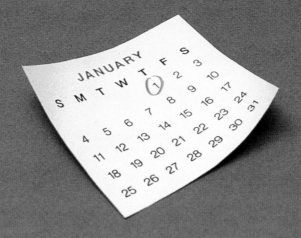

new year's day brunch

MENU

LUCKY BLACK-EYED PEAS
AND CHORIZO SALAD

THERE'S NO PLACE LIKE HOME FRIES

CITRUS-MINT FRUIT SALAD

POACHED EGGS WITH CREAMED SPINACH
AND ARTICHOKE HEARTS

ALMOND CROISSANT FRENCH TOAST

TRULY THE BEST BLOODY MARYS

HANGOVER HELPER

A soothing brunch for recovering revelers

IT'S NEW YEAR'S DAY. Do you know where your pots and pans are? If not, find them, because this is an ideal day for cooking. First of all, it's cold outside and no one wants to be anywhere but someplace warm and cozy, at a home-cooked brunch with friends, or in the coziest place of all, a nice warm food coma. Second, since it's likely your wallet is empty after the previous evening's festivities, having friends over for a casual meal around the fireplace is the perfect way to entertain without breaking the bank. Third and perhaps most important is that your future depends on it. In order to have good luck in the new year, superstition in the South holds, you must eat black-eyed peas on New Year's Day. Since you're not likely to find them on many restaurant menus (not in Manhattan anyway), the only way to be certain of their availability is to cook them yourself. Or, as we did, make Becky promise to bring her warm black-eyed peas and chorizo salad. It was so good that Katherine tried to convince us of an obscure addendum to the superstition: "The more black-eyed peas you stuff into your piehole, the luckier you'll be." Does this saying really exist? No, of course it doesn't. But we humored her, and our bellies, and had second helpings.

Since New Year's Day is undisputedly the mother of mornings-after, we created a menu scientifically engineered to soothe any possible ailment and satisfy every craving— from poached eggs with creamed spinach and artichoke hearts, to home fries with bacon, to a citrus-mint fruit salad. Maybe it's not exactly scientific, but it certainly did the job for this

Cooking Club. Our Almond Croissant French Toast alone will make your guests wish they were hungover every morning.

Aside from remembering not to be frightened by this beyond-decadent meal (you earned it—New Year's Eve is hard work!), the real key to this party is to keep it casual and comfortable. For instance, Sharon's baby daughter, Margot, had the right idea and came clad in a turquoise velour baby sweatsuit. So think couches, comfy chairs, and that J. Crew sweater you secretly envisioned yourself wearing to a cozy get-together just like this one. And since this is a day when no one wants to wake up early to prepare numerous courses, this is the perfect party for a cooking club or to throw as a potluck. Don't fuss with decorations, either. Simply throw some pillows on the floor, turn on a football game, and assure guests they'll be woken up in time for French toast if they fall asleep between courses.

START THE YEAR OFF RIGHT

1. Set out a bowl of Advil, Pepto-Bismol, and any other rough-morning remedies that you have on hand. Your guests will love you for it. Plus, it's better than having them sneaking off midbrunch to go rummage around in your medicine cabinet.

2. Play the fortune game: Write out fortunes on pieces of paper and fold them in half. (Example: "This year you will find a new love, join a cooking club, and possibly meet Oprah Winfrey.") Fill a large serving bowl with water and arrange the folded papers around the rim. Use melted wax to affix a small candle to the inside of a plastic bottle top. Have each guest take a turn dropping the lighted candle "boat" into the center of the bowl of water. Whichever paper their candle drifts toward is their fortune.

3. This is exactly the kind of day that fireplaces were made for, so let 'er rip. Assign someone to the role of "fireplace DJ" so you don't have to check on it continually throughout the party. And if you lack a fireplace, but still want to create "fireplace ambience," put out a basket of fragrant pinecones, or simply invite guests to take turns pulling a chair up next to your stove.

JANUARY

new year's day brunch

LUCKY BLACK-EYED PEAS AND CHORIZO SALAD

Not only will eating this salad make you lucky, but the beans in this salad should consider themselves lucky as well—after all, who wouldn't feel fortunate being cozied up next to succulent pieces of spicy chorizo sausage on a cold New Year's morning? ■ *Yield: 4 to 6 servings*

2 15-ounce cans black-eyed peas, drained and rinsed
8 scallions, chopped
½ cup coarsely chopped fresh parsley

FOR THE DRESSING
1 teaspoon dried marjoram
1 teaspoon cumin
1 tablespoon smooth Dijon mustard
2 cloves garlic, finely chopped
2 tablespoons red wine vinegar
¼ cup extra-virgin olive oil

—

1 pound chorizo sausage, cut into ¼-inch slices
salt and freshly ground pepper to taste

I   Combine the peas, scallions, and parsley in a large bowl.
2   In a small bowl, combine the marjoram, cumin, mustard, garlic, and vinegar. Whisk in the olive oil in a slow stream to emulsify. Add the dressing to the peas mixture and toss. Set aside.
3   Cook the sausage in a large skillet over medium heat until cooked through. Add the sausage to the peas mixture. Season with salt and pepper. Serve immediately while still warm, or at room temperature.

THERE'S NO PLACE LIKE HOME FRIES

Not only did Dorothy give us the go-ahead to wear red sequined pumps during the day, but she also gave us the wonderful piece of wisdom. And she was right, there is no place like home. Especially if home is where fried potatoes are served for breakfast. We even added crumbled bacon to ours. Yes, you read right, bacon. No need to thank us, just consider it a little holiday gift from us to you. ■ *Yield: 6 servings*

8 slices bacon

1 large yellow onion, chopped

2 pounds baking potatoes, peeled and cut
into ¼-inch cubes

1½ teaspoons chopped fresh rosemary or
½ teaspoon dried rosemary

salt and freshly ground pepper to taste

I   Fry the bacon in a large skillet until crispy. Remove onto paper towels. Do not discard the bacon grease. When the bacon is cool enough to handle, crumble into coarse pieces and set aside.

2   Over high heat, sauté the onion and potatoes in the bacon grease left in the skillet, stirring frequently. Cook until the potatoes are golden brown. Add the rosemary; season with salt and pepper. Stir in the crumbled bacon. Serve immediately.

new year's day brunch

CITRUS-MINT FRUIT SALAD

This fruit salad is perfect for your New Year's brunch because the chopped mint will be a bracing slap to your sorry, drunkard face. (Er, sorry, Becky insisted we write that.) What we really meant to say is that the honey and citrus are a lovely balance of sweet and tart, and the fresh mint leaves are a delightfully refreshing addition to this fruit salad. ■ *Yield: 6 servings*

1 large grapefruit

5 oranges (any combination of navel orange, blood orange, and tangerine)

4 green kiwis

3 teaspoons honey

3 tablespoons chopped fresh mint

1 Peel the grapefruit, oranges, and kiwis. Separate the grapefruit and oranges into segments over a medium bowl to catch the juices. Set the juice aside and put the segments in a separate, large serving bowl.

2 Slice the kiwis horizontally into ⅛-inch-thick rounds. Cut the rounds into halves and add to the grapefruit and orange segments.

3 Whisk the honey into the bowl with the juice. Pour the honey-juice mixture over the fruit in the large bowl. Add the mint; toss. Keep refrigerated until ready to serve.

POACHED EGGS WITH CREAMED SPINACH AND ARTICHOKE HEARTS

When Cynthia arrived at our New Year's Day brunch, she was clearly hurting. She had danced until dawn and as a result was now living in a big ol' house of pain. But after only one bite of these restorative eggs, she miraculously rose from the sofa and, the next thing we knew, was doing something that could only be described as a "happy robot" dance. The point is, these eggs have the power to get your motor running. ■ *Yield: Six 1-egg portions*

1½ pounds fresh spinach
3 tablespoons unsalted butter
2½ tablespoons all-purpose flour
1½ cups milk
½ cup shredded Jarlsberg cheese
½ cup shredded Gruyère cheese
1½ cups coarsely chopped canned artichoke hearts, drained

½ teaspoon Tabasco Sauce
½ teaspoon salt
½ teaspoon freshly ground pepper
1 tablespoon vinegar
6 eggs
paprika for garnish

1   Wash the spinach in cold water. Cut and discard the stems. Place the wet spinach leaves in a large saucepan. Cover and cook over medium heat for 3 minutes. Drain well and squeeze dry. Set aside.

2   Melt the butter in a small saucepan over low heat. Gradually add the flour, whisking constantly for 2 minutes. Gradually whisk in the milk. Increase the heat to medium-low, whisking constantly for 3 to 4 minutes, until mixture has thickened. Add the cheeses and stir until melted. Remove from the heat. Reserve ¾ cup of the sauce; transfer the remaining sauce to a blender or food processor. Add the spinach and blend together. Return the mixture to a saucepan and stir in the artichoke hearts, Tabasco Sauce, salt, and pepper.

3   Bring 4 cups water and the vinegar to a simmer in a large skillet. Break 1 egg into a cup and gently slip into the water. Cook for 2 minutes, or until the egg is set but the yolk is still runny. Remove with a slotted spoon and put into a bowl of warm water until ready to serve. Repeat with the remaining 5 eggs.

4   When ready to serve, reheat the spinach mixture over low heat and reheat the reserved ¾ cup cheese sauce in a small saucepan. Add milk, if needed, to thin out the sauce. Divide the spinach mixture among 6 plates. Place 1 egg on each spinach bed. Top the eggs with the sauce. Sprinkle with paprika. Serve immediately.

new year's day brunch

YOU CAN KEEP THIS
BAKED FRENCH
TOAST WARM IN THE
OVEN UNTIL YOUR
GUESTS ARRIVE

ALMOND CROISSANT FRENCH TOAST

None of us will ever forget the sight of Lisa coming out of the kitchen with a casserole dish of this French toast, enveloped in a halo of buttery almond goodness. Katherine (who has clearly read *Gone With the Wind* a few too many times) likes to say that at that moment, Lisa was our Melanie, a vision of pure, angelic kindness coming to the aid of her wounded soldiers. OK, so New Year's Eve isn't exactly the Civil War, but this French toast really may cause hallucinations. Lucia claims that after one bite she saw herself in a field of almond trees, running with her arms open toward a giant stick of butter. Our new mom, Sharon, said simply that it was as lovely as an epidural. ▪ *Yield: 6 servings*

7 large eggs	½ teaspoon grated lemon zest
2½ cups milk	1 teaspoon almond extract
2½ tablespoons sugar	8 medium croissants
1 teaspoon vanilla extract	maple syrup
6 tablespoons (¾ stick) unsalted butter	powdered sugar
½ cup sliced raw almonds	

1 Preheat the oven to 325 degrees. Spray a deep 13-by-9-inch baking dish with cooking spray.

2 In a large bowl, beat the eggs, then whisk in the milk, granulated sugar, and vanilla extract. Set aside.

3 In a small saucepan, melt the butter. Add the almond slices, lemon zest, and almond extract.

4 Cut the croissants in half horizontally. Place 8 halves, cut side up, in the prepared baking dish. Drizzle 1 heaping teaspoon of the almond mixture onto each croissant. Place the remaining 8 croissant halves, cut side down, in the dish to form a second layer. (The top halves should not line up perfectly with the halves on the bottom layer.) Pour the egg mixture evenly on top of the croissants.

5 Drizzle the remaining almond mixture on top of the croissants. Bake, uncovered, for about 35 minutes, until puffed and set. Allow to cool a few minutes before cutting pieces. Serve with maple syrup and/or powdered sugar.

new year's day brunch

CYNTHIA AND
LISA STEP INTO
THE NEW YEAR

TRULY THE BEST BLOODY MARYS

Has the Cooking Club ever lied to you? Exactly. So believe us when we tell you that these are truly the best Bloody Marys. Katherine's dad is the source for this recipe, and he doesn't mess around when it comes to this beloved hair-of-the-dog beverage. But here's what you have to remember: The lemon juice has to be fresh and the celery salt is a must. And if, after that, you still don't believe that these are in fact the best Bloody Marys you've ever tasted, you should probably keep it to yourself—Katherine's dad is a big man. ■ *Yield: 6 drinks*

1 quart tomato juice
½ cup fresh lemon juice
3 tablespoons Worcestershire sauce
2 tablespoons bottled horseradish
(more if you want them spicier)
¼ teaspoon garlic powder
½ teaspoon celery salt
freshly cracked pepper to taste
several drops of Tabasco Sauce
6 jiggers vodka

FOR THE GARNISH
celery salt
ice cubes
celery stalks, pickled green beans, or pickled okra

1 Mix all the ingredients together in a pitcher, except for the vodka and those for the garnish. The mixture can be kept refrigerated for up to 1 day.
2 When ready to serve, stir in the vodka.
3 Salt the rims of 6 highball glasses with celery salt and fill each with ice. Pour in the Bloody Mary mixture and add garnish.

new year's day brunch

INDEX

THE COOKING CLUB

KATHERINE FAUSSET is the member least likely to be attacked by vampires. Her cooking motto: Always add more garlic. Having survived countless Mardi Gras parties in her hometown of New Orleans, Katherine showed us the finer points of hangover recovery at our New Year's Day brunch. We count on her to bring to every party her well-seasoned cuisine, an appetite for all things shrimp- or oyster-related, her own bottle of Tabasco Sauce, and, if the occasion demands it, an enormous hat. **Favorite CC member:** Sharon's baby, Margot.

SHARON COHEN FREDMAN is the only member who has made an entire holiday family dinner by herself. She will tell you that roasting a turkey while preparing all the sides and desserts is not entirely unlike giving birth. Because Sharon is the first member to have a child, it has been unanimously decided by the rest of the club that little Margot is indeed the most adorable baby in the world. **Most memorable moment:** Known for her low-fat fare, Sharon stunned the group when she unveiled jumbo ice cream sandwiches, then announced her pregnancy.

REBECCA SAMPLE GERSTUNG chose her apartment not only for its spacious kitchen but also for its soundproof walls, rendering the possibility of getting evicted due to loud and unruly karaoke parties obsolete. Known for finding obscure (and, quite frankly, large) party-seating such as Hawaiian-print patio chairs and vintage orange beanbags for club members to kick back on, she can convert almost any meal into fondue. **Dream food:** a cheese ball wrapped in cheese smothered in cheese sauce.

As our book designer, food stylist, and source of endless luau props, CYNTHIA HARRIS is known for mixing style with sustenance. A firm believer that food should be aesthetically pleasing to the eye as well as the palate, she's also our resident Garnish Goddess, armed with freshly chopped chives to sprinkle on a dish at a moment's notice. When she's not perfecting the marshmallow figure-eight swirl in her Chocolate Fluffer Fondue, she's usually begging Becky to break out the karaoke machine. **CC fantasy:** gingerbread Taj Mahal with gelatin reflecting pool.

LUCIA QUARTARARO MULDER, the monstermind behind CC's spine-tingling Halloween soirees, defends her title of Liquid Pleasure Director and adds Ghoulish Gourmand to her résumé thanks to a tendency to make food that stares back at you with spooky edible eyes. The timing of her recent wedding subjected her to much Cooking Club celebratory experimentation, and she eagerly awaits revisiting some of these new "traditions" when the time comes. **Earliest matrimonial test:** hosting the entire club for the weekend.

The consummate hostess, LISA SINGER single-handedly turned a potentially stuffy Kentucky Derby party into a fantastic fete, procuring both fancy hats *and* Jim Beam flasks for all members. Known as CC's mother figure, she is often seen holding our train tickets or dispensing Advil from her purse. A recovering candy addict, Lisa has been known to finish off an Almond Joy with a Reese's chaser. **Biggest decor coup:** procuring our very first piñata for Mexican Night.